Walter Savage Landor

By ERNEST DILWORTH
Lehigh University

Twayne Publishers, Inc.   : :   New York

PREFACE

This book about Walter Savage Landor is in no sense a biography, nor is it meant to be an outline of his works. The reader in search of paraphrase will find enough of it in John Forster's life. There, and in Mr. R. H. Super's biography and other studies, he will find his facts. My purpose has been to write a critical study and, at the same time, an introduction to the delights offered readers by a stylist of great distinction. I have wanted to recount what Landor tried to do and to discover what he did well, to describe the experience of reading him, and to arrive at some conclusions about his art and the mind it expresses. The subject naturally requires some discussion of the relationship between form and matter and between the quality of a man's words and the quality of the thing he says.

In a study of the prose and verse of a fine writer whose work is little known, quotation will of necessity be profuse; perhaps it will also be welcome. Incidentally, very many of Landor's poems have no regular titles and are known only by their first lines. I have therefore relegated a title to the notes when its appearance in the text would have been awkward.

In preparing a chronology, I have had the advantage not only of Sidney Colvin's in his volume of selections prepared for the Golden Treasury Series but of that of Mr. Malcolm Elwin. Permission to quote from Stephen Wheeler's edition of *Landor's Poetical Works* has been granted by the Clarendon Press. I have enjoyed the use of the Lehigh University and Princeton University libraries and of the great institution of Inter-Library Loan. I here publish my thanks to my mother, Edith Johnson Dilworth, for much yeoman service in proofreading; to my sisters, Nancy Johnson and Sylvia Fichtel, on general principles; and to my friend and more than once collaborator, Walter Leuba, who gave and lent me Landoriana. I think I'll dedicate this book to the four of them.

E. N. DILWORTH

CONTENTS

CHRONOLOGY

1775 Walter Savage Landor, born at Warwick, January 30.

1779–
1780 At school at Knowle.

1783 To Rugby.

1791 Brought home from Rugby.

1792 Tutored at Ashbourne, Derbyshire, under Reverend William Langley.

1793 To Trinity College, Oxford.

1794 Rusticated.

1795 Living in London. *The Poems of Walter Savage Landor*.

1796–
1797 Wales and Warwick. Met Rose Aylmer.

1798–
1801 Bath, London, Swansea, Warwick. *Gebir* (1798).

1800 *Poems from the Arabic and Persian. Iambi*.

1802 *Poetry by the Author of Gebir*. Visit to Paris.

1803–
1807 Bath and elsewhere (movements now uncertain). 1803, met Jane Sophia Swift (Ianthe).

1805 Death of father, November 3.

1806 *Simonidea*.

1808 Purchased Llanthony Abbey. Met Robert Southey. In Spain as volunteer (August–October).

1809–
1813 Llanthony and Bath.

1811 Married Julia Thuillier, May 24.

1812 *Count Julian*.

1814 Left his wife in Jersey. Tours.

1815 Rejoined by wife at Tours. Met Francis Hare. Como. *Idyllia*.

1816–
1818 Como.

1818　Como, Genoa, Pisa. Birth of eldest son Arnold (Como, March 5).

1820　Pisa. *Idyllia Heroica*. Birth of daughter Julia (March 6).

1821–
1828　Florence: Palazzo Medici, 1821–26.

1822　Fifteen new dialogues finished (letter to Southey, March 9). Birth of second son Walter (November 13).

1824　*Imaginary Conversations of Literary Men and Statesmen,* 2 vols. Arrangements owing to Julius Hare.

1825　Birth of third son Charles (August 5).

1826　Visited Rome with Francis Hare (a month, January–February). Autumn: moved to Via de' Pandolfini.

1827　Met Lord and Lady Blessington. Moved (summer) to Villa Castiglione.

1828　*Imaginary Conversations,* Vol. III.

1829–
1835　Fiesole: Villa Gherardesca, bought in 1829. *Imaginary Conversations,* Vols. IV and V.

1831　*Gebir, Count Julian, and other Poems.*

1832　Trip to England.

1833　Visited by Ralph Waldo Emerson in Fiesole.

1834　*Citation and Examination of William Shakespeare.*

1835　Left wife and children at Fiesole. Lucca. England.

1836　Clifton. *Pericles and Aspasia,* 2 vols. In Germany for three months in hopes of seeing his children. Met John Forster.

1837　*The Pentameron and Pentalogia.* Bath: 35 St. James's Square, until April, 1844.

1839　*Andrea of Hungary,* and *Giovanna of Naples.*

1841　*Fra Rupert.*

1842　Visit of his son Arnold (June–September).

1843　Visit of Walter and Julia.

1844　(April) Moved to 1 St. James's Square, Bath (until 1846).

1846　(September) Moved to 42 St. James's Square, Bath (until December), then to No. 36 (until April, 1849). *The Works of Walter Savage Landor,* 2 vols.

1847　*Hellenics; Poemata et Inscriptiones.*

1848　*Italics. Imaginary Conversation of King Carlo-Alberto and the Duchess Belgioioso* for the benefit of the sufferers from the bombardment of Messina. Began a seven-year series of letters on foreign affairs in the *Examiner.*

1849　Moved (April) to 3 Rivers Street, Bath (until 1858).

Chronology

CHAPTER 1

Biographical

WALTER Savage Landor never did anything by halves. From childhood to the day of his death, he was a scorner of compromise. He threw himself into life, and he was a great partisan of contemplative retirement. Avid of calmness and helplessly passionate, he was ferocious in guarding his privacy and published his most intimate feelings. A great burst of temper, in him, would be followed by a great burst of laughter. He tolerated nothing that seemed to him an injustice, and injustices ran at his heels. Touchily proud and untamably independent, he was sympathetic and generous to a degree. He adored the soft grace of young girls and recommended tyrannicide as a virtue. He wasted a fortune trying to build the greatest estate in Wales, and he wrote four volumes of verse as an avocation. He spoiled his children and perfected his prose.

None of the above need be seen as paradoxical; it all comes from a strong sense of life, and sometimes the pulse is louder than the judgment. When young, he rejoiced in rudeness; as he matured, he found pleasure in amenity. Yet the courtly old man could be a tiger. He seldom fell into physical violence, but his moral pugnacity was alarming. He lived in words, and his battles were fought with ideas; considering the scrapes he got into, it was always a wonder that he had never had to fight a duel, but it was said that his eccentricity saved him.

At sixteen he was sent home from Rugby for being rebellious and no respector of persons. He had been there for eight years, and he remained a legend for his arrogant wit and the brilliance of his

Latin verses. He remembered Rugby with tenderness as the place where he grew, in mind and body, in poetry and in friendship.

After private tutoring he went to Trinity College, Oxford, where he studied deeply and continued to write, in both Greek and Latin. One evening, following a row between a party in his rooms and a party across the way, Landor fired a volley of small shot against the closed shutters opposite him. As a result, he was rusticated for two terms; Landor was nineteen; he never went back. In a few months he was in London, continuing his studies independently, and having his poems published. It was 1795, he was twenty; his private life had begun.

It was truly a life rather than a career. The first two volumes of *Imaginary Conversations* were not published until he was forty-nine, and soon afterward he had quietly become a kind of classic. He had been having his work printed for thirty years, and there had been no rise in estimation, no rocketing, no fame. He was simply known and valued by a sufficient number of persons who cared for good writing. He was perfectly aware that he was little read, and he had the sense to make no effort at popularity. Ralph Waldo Emerson said, in his essay on Landor in *The Dial* (October, 1841), "Now for twenty years we have still found the 'Imaginary Conversations' a sure resource in solitude, and it seems to us as original in its form as in its matter." He referred to Landor's "rich and ample page." [1] Nevertheless, he could speak of "the haughtiness of Landor's Muse content to please himself, for who the devil is the reader?" [2] To please himself was not Landor's only literary principle, but it was a reasonable one, and he kept at it until he was nearly ninety: no career, no program, no progress, no fads —only loving craftsmanship and the hope of wisdom.

The death of his father enabled him to pursue the plans of a prince: in Wales, as the transformer of Llanthony Abbey; in Spain, as a volunteer against the French, more than paying his way. He left Spain as an honorary colonel and Wales as a defeated civilian; in both campaigns he let officialdom know what he thought of them. Meanwhile, he wrote poems and political pamphlets. It is a question whether during his whole life he fulminated more over politics or property. At any rate, he did not smart without protest, and he was as pleased to excoriate a duke or an emperor as a mere neighbor who troubled his peace.

In full consciousness of the dramatic value of his gesture, he married a pretty girl who had no money. The pretty girl, Julia

Thuillier, could not keep pace with his noble stride, was uninterested in his mind, and balked at his humors; she pitied herself, became a shrew, and at last made him a cuckold.

Three years after his marriage he had tried to wash himself clean of Wales and of various lawsuits by crossing to the Continent. His wife decided to forgive him for his age and his other faults and followed him. He published some new idyls in Latin, but his own were over. And yet it must be added that a certain pristine sweetness survived in him to the end, so that the bitterness of his family life was always to be alleviated by new and innocent affections.

He began writing the *Imaginary Conversations* in 1821, in Florence, where in one house or another he lived for eight years before buying the Villa Gherardesca, a little east of San Domenico, below Fiesole, in the country of the *Decameron*. "Here," he wrote to Robert Southey, "I shall pass my life; long or short, no matter. . . ." [3] When in 1835 he left his wife, his three sons, and his daughter and returned alone to England, he was sixty years old and unregretted. His children, on whom he had poured unstinted affection, chose to stay with their mother, whose railing, often in company, and disloyal conduct could no longer be borne by a husband. Landor had not been wise in his dealings with family or neighbors, but that he was neither a fool nor a brute is borne witness to by the friends who never gave him up.

He settled in Bath, on a small income he reserved for himself, and lived there for twenty-one years, regularly visiting friends in the country or in London. At the age of eighty-two, in a fury at injustice to a young woman, he attacked in print, and beyond all reason, an older woman named Mrs. Yescombe. Entangled in a libel case, he left England for the last time. His family, at the Villa Landor, did not welcome him; and at eighty-four, he walked, like Lear, out of the house that was no longer his and stumbled through the heat to Florence. Robert Browning, who met him in the street, took him in. Landor was then established in rooms in town, where he continued to write prose and verse and to see old and new friends. In his last year, his younger sons Charles and Walter were decent enough to attend to his physical needs. Six months before he died, the young Algernon Swinburne paid him his never-to-be-forgotten visit of homage. Landor had wanted to be buried in Widcombe churchyard near Bath; but he lies in the locked English cemetery in Florence, a bulging island in a sea of traffic.

The unused epitaph that Landor wrote for himself carries under his name and dates these words only: "His Friends were, until death, Southey, Francis, Julius and Augustus Hare, G. P. R. James, and Gen. W. Napier." [4] He was happy in other dear friends until their death or his, among them Walter Birch, of Rugby and Oxford days; Joseph Ablett; John Kenyon; the comtesse de Molandé (Ianthe); Lady Graves Sawle (niece of Rose Aylmer); Browning, who for five years watched over his affairs; and Lady Blessington, whose homes were always his. Through her he met Charles Dickens, who put aspects of him into *Bleak House* as Boythorn. Though Landor saw Dickens less often than some, Dickens's affectionate understanding of Landor was worthy of them both. "You see many I daresay," said Dickens in a letter in 1856, "and hear from many I have no doubt, who love you heartily; but we silent people in the distance never forget you. . . . I write to you so often in my books." [5]

Looking, from a distance, at Landor's occasional wild behavior, well-behaved men have comfortably assured the world, as Leslie Stephen did, that, whatever else he was, Landor was a schoolboy all his life.[6] "The taunt is stale," said Swinburne angrily in a letter to Sidney Colvin; and he called Stephen's essay on Landor "a very type . . . of floundering acuteness and blundering insight that sees many things keenly and most of them wrongly. . . ." [7] Swinburne's criticism, in spite of his warm partisanship, is just; but it would be difficult to make many people see the floundering of such Olympian, such terribly assured and measured acuteness as that of Sir Leslie Stephen.

Our subject is no Olympian. He is one of the imperfect creatures of the world we know. As a person, he was dramatically unique. To Browning, he was "a man who, in spite of strange mistakings, and unfortunate hastinesses of judgment and temper, was gifted with more extraordinary endowments, as well of heart as of head, than ever met in a man before,—so far as my experience goes." [8] To his family, he was a phenomenon that in the end merited a hackneyed inscription on a gravestone: "Sacred/to the Memory of/Walter Savage Landor/born 30th day of January 1775/died on the 17th of September 1864./ This last sad tribute/of his wife and children." [9] Sad indeed—but the man left works behind him.

CHAPTER 2

Verse: The Heroic

I The Nature of Amusement

"POETRY," said Walter Landor to Archdeacon Hare, in the imaginary conversation between the two of them, "Poetry was always my amusement; prose my study and business." [1] No doubt, in making this distinction Landor was first of all protecting himself; he who drank deep and habitually of Milton, and who had always fed on the great writing of the past, was not wholly deceived about his own powers. In friendship, his feelings carried him away; but one of the things this study may show is that Landor was capable of criticizing his own work.

It would be foolish, however, to underestimate the weight of his word "amusement." The persistence of puritanism causes a great many speakers of English to look upon amusement as something soothingly amoral and unintellectual. Amusement or enjoyment is seen literally as relaxation—as an unstrung state in which consciousness meanders or lies down, is required no longer to choose; for judgment and choice are morality, and morality is on vacation. That judgment and choice are the very life of consciousness, and that they are a pleasure, and that pleasure itself must bud and flower in the warm light of mind, are truths almost inconceivable by our latter-day puritans (I had almost said Romantics). Only the mind is capable of amusement, and it can find in what appears mere physical labor the satisfactions of art. The writing of verse was amusement to Landor because he craved such satisfactions.

From boyhood at Rugby, where the excellence of his Latin verses won half-holiday for him and for his schoolmates, Landor had practiced the craft; for one does not suddenly or by accident acquire the facility and grace of his juvenilia. And the practice went on into his ninetieth year. He was first and last a maker, a poet in the oldest sense; even before breakfast, even on his daily walks, he was forever putting together sentences in verse or in prose, trying them against his remarkable ear. Hardly anything happened to him that he was willing to let go before he had tried to crystallize it in words. He needed, like Picasso or William Morris, to be always working. Passing pleasures and irritations lost their visceral imprecision in becoming verse. Form made its demands to the extent that verses forced themselves into his conversation, into his letters—and between lines of finished prose.

This verbal energy was not professionalism but simple creativity; of another man we might say, "He must always be doing something with his hands." The satisfactions of doing something in verse are evident enough; but, when one rounds out a sentence in prose, turns it, polishes it, perfects it—someone asks how one meant to go on from there! A perfect sentence in prose always appears to be a fragment of some longer work, just as a book of maxims, however beautiful in themselves, seems a collection of favorite passages. A poem, on the other hand, is so vitally a lone object it is almost a creature. It is something done but not done with, for it continues to draw us back to it, and so to life. That poor perfect sentence in prose may be poetry itself, but, alas, we know what a poem should look like.

For a born maker, what could be more natural than to write verses or whittle sticks, to hit upon new melodies in the bath or old delights in the kitchen? But if the maker is ambitious; if he is moved by an excess of energy, a proud restlessness of mind—if, in short, he is one capable of saying, "When men strike at genius, they strike at the face of God in the only way wherein he ever manifests it to them," [2] he has made a remark to remember—and one, by the way, to compare with other remarks about greatness in which he will be more classically self-contained. Such a man, at least, finds something he can do better than anyone else, though the perfection make a solitude around him.

II *Early Struggles with Verse*

Such a man will not feel his way; he will strike out boldly. To write Latin verses (as Landor did throughout his lifetime) is, in recent centuries, an indulgence, a civilized amusement, rather than a proof of genius. At the age of twenty, Landor published in three books, only one of them in Latin, *The Poems of Walter Savage Landor*.

The first of these poems is a lucubration entitled "The Birth of Poesy," in three cantos (it was meant to be finished in five). In our own day, the young man who wants to prove that he can write tries a novel; the older tradition called for an epic or a long essay in verse. There is little doubt which test is the more stringent. Landor, moreover, chose to do his essay in the heroic couplet. Blank verse could come later, as the boar hunt might be proper after he had slain his first dragon. "The Birth of Poesy" is no more dense and unreadable than most efforts of the sort. It is unoriginal; it contains, of course, many reminders of the poet's own reading. Milton is there, with a voluminous serpent and with Adam and Eve: "Their eyes reverting oft, they slowly went, Hand claspt in hand, to wander and repent."[3] James Thomson, as a pallid apparition, seems to be with us for a moment:

> But when fierce Winter vexes them with cold,
> Nor banks nor dams the violent surge can hold:
> The fearful Shepherd, at a distance, sees
> His flooded folds and insulated trees:
> His flocks, in haste, their wonted vallies fly,
> Or in the waters overwhelmed die.[4]

Perhaps it was William Cowper on the arm of Thomson—but dim, very dim. Somewhat more promising, entirely because of its last line, is the following from Landor's Canto III:

> Thus, throughout nature every part affords
> More sound instruction than from *winged words*.
> By me more felt, more studied, than the rules
> Of Pedants strutting in sophistic schools;
> Who argumentative, with endless strife,
> In search of living lose the ends of life.
> Or willing exiles from fair Pleasure's train,
> Howl at the happy from the dens of Pain.[5]

That last line reflects a flash of joy in the subject; we catch it in the choice of "howl," the alliterative contrast of "happy," and the free but certain rhythm. (In another sense of freedom, young Landor is fond of Alexandrines, some of which are not needless, but happily draw out the idea, as in this from "Abelard to Eloise": "No Eloise hails their morn, no cloister dims their days." [6]

In metrics the young poet shows real skill, from pentameter and tetrameter couplets and quatrains (of the poems in tetrameter couplet, some are comic and some not) to his use (in "The French Villagers") of the *In Memoriam* stanza well before Tennyson. The subject matter is varied and not crazily miscellaneous: there are a "Pyramus and Thisbe," an "Ode on the Departure of Mary, Queen of Scots, from France," an "Ode to General Washington"; there is an "Apology for Satire"; there are Stanzas "written by the water-side" and imitations from Catullus. Most of the poetry is that of a very young versifier, and too little of it from a very young man who says anything he very much wanted to say. We are treated to a "pensive Collins," a "modest Addison," and a "brave Dundas." [7] Prizes tend to be "palmy." [8] In one case the young man makes an obvious effort at verbal agility—"The dear, the dread, ubiquity of love" [9]—and, because the aim was unworthy, the effort will not do. Finally, there are "daisy pied" and "modest violet," [10] which are all too typical of these remarkably fluent efforts, whose versification already is second nature to the versifier.

Mastery of the shopworn phraseology of one's own time is mental servitude—but it is not a hopeless state if the master is young, or if he shows signs of discovering himself and the words that belong to and reveal that self. And it should be said that, though a poem may bore us with "the generous tear" and "the sprightly dance," it may offer us—and "The French Villagers" does offer us, as part of old men's memories of youth—something fresher: "The leering eye, the damask red,/The ringlets that enticed to toy." In all these phrases, the definite article calls before us broadly familiar, evocative representative pictures, as it was meant to do.

Yet none of this work, except for the expert management of versification, manages to be very complimentary to young Landor. Where these poems are weak it is because of the poet's distance from the object; there is nothing stupid or disgusting about them. Furthermore, there are signs of real writing, moments when his diction shows that he has drawn near his object and has participated in its way of being. There is "Robin—with retorted eye" [11] and the primrose, which in the morning "Sips the lively stream of light." [12] And, on what most people might call the more intellectual side of imagination, Landor's epigrammatic instinct began to show itself early, as in these two examples from this 1795 volume.

ON A QUAKER'S TANKARD
Ye lie, friend Pindar! and friend Thales!
Nothing so good as water? Ale is.

EXPLANATION OF A GREEK PROVERB
"Gods play at ball with us poor men."
—Thus an outrageous Sophist ran on—
Kings, who do *now,* what Gods did *then,*
To save their fingers call for cannon.

Although we find better verse as time goes on, the skill evinced is a rare one. For a summary view of what his accomplishment already was, I quote a few lines from his "Moral Epistle" of the same year: [13]

But turn we round: behold how swiftly flies
The mist illusive that obscured our eyes!
Throned on a mountain, down whose side is roll'd
A rapid torrent tinged with sands of gold:
Whose barren height projects a chilly shade
O'er every cottage in the nether glade:
Where sleepless hellebore and bitter rue
Forbid the bee to sip their vernal dew:
Where nightshade twines the bower, and hemloc grows
With proud luxuriance round the wither'd rose—
Sits haggard Avarice! with bloody hand
She grasps the sceptre of supreme command.

His youthfulness does not show, as it could not help doing if he wrote in a tradition of exhibitionistic individualism. The work is literate, civilized, decorative work-for-work's-sake; it is technically mature—and melodious.

III   *The Larger-than-life:* Gebir

Three years later was published *Gebir,* and the improvement, as is the way in youth, is striking—not in construction or in technique, but in poetry. Clara Reeve had published at the end of her *Progress of Romance* (1785) "The History of Charoba, Queen of Egypt," drawn from an Arabian history of ancient Egypt. The story, in no matter whose version, tells of the imposing young king *Gebir* of

Gades (Cadiz), who fulfills an old promise to conquer Egypt; of the love that surprises Gebir and the conquered Queen Charoba; and of his assassination at the time of what seems their merely political marriage. Landor's *Gebir* is printed under "Heroic Poems" in Stephen Wheeler's edition; Clara Reeve would call it a romance, which she defines as *"an Heroic fable,*—a fabulous Story of such actions as are commonly ascribed to heroes, or men of extraordinary courage and abilities." [14] Landor calls it a poem, but he conceives it as a heroic tragic one.

Of the most important changes Landor makes in the tale, two are epic in intent: Gebir visits the underworld; and the shepherd who wrestles with the nymph becomes Gebir's brother Tamar, with a complete story of his own, and even a whole book to himself so that, Aeneas-like, he may be seen as the father of a future country spreading from the Garonne to the Rhine. All this ambitious mimicry of heroic literary example is interesting, as well as irrelevant to what proclaims itself as the burden of the plot: conquest ending in love, and death supervening by a last, delayed convulsion of violence. The work is ill-planned and often obscure, but it is worth reading with patience; for, if it is a failure, there is much poetry in it, and it bears, throughout 1,900 lines, marks of nobility and none of disgrace.

The story develops in the pauses of pageantry, and we must often infer its direction from the musings of Gebir and Charoba, each in a cloudy solitude. Gebir himself, I find I do not know at all; Charoba, I both see and understand in flashes. The vanquished normally arouse men's sympathy; in this poem, they draw the poet away from his hero. The feelings of Charoba are described at some length, and she rises and sits before us as on a stage. We are helped by what her nurse Dalica tells us of the past; breathless but determined, old Dalica confesses that " 'compar'd with Youth/Age has a something something like repose' " She is here speaking to her sister Myrthyr (most foul) the sorceress:

> Twelve years ago Charoba first could speak.
> If her indulgent father asked her name,
> She would indulge him too, and would reply
> *"What? why, Charoba"*—rais'd with sweet surprize,
> And proud to shine teacher in her turn.
> . . . .
> She thought the crown a plaything to amuse

> Herself, and not the people, for she thought
> Who mimick infant words might infant toys:
> But while she watched grave elders look with awe
> On such a bauble, she withheld her breath;
> She was afraid her parents should suspect
> They had caught childhood from her in a kiss. . .[15]

The soul of Charoba has changed, says Dalica, under the spell of Gebir. On her first view of the ocean "She coldly said, her long-lash'd eyes abased,/'Is this the mighty ocean? is this all!' " [16] That capacious soul, once "discontented with capacity," [17] is gone. She has become a girl; and, in her wild grief at the sudden death of Gebir, she is a girl still, calling the name of her mother. Her raving itself shows the delicacy of mind that was to make Landor incapable of rant. The finest of these lines is touched with memory of the love of parents and children: "Where are ye, dear fond parents! when ye heard/My feet in childhood pat the palace floor,/Ye started forth, and kist away surprize." [18] But more in key with the work as a whole are the splendid lines describing the multitudes, struck mute:

> —the feast
> Was like the feast of Cepheus, when the sword
> Of Phineus, white with wonder, shook restrain'd,
> And the hilt rattled in his marble hand.[19]

Not many people bought or read *Gebir*. Southey was given it to review, was delighted with it, and became Landor's friend for life, and the friends of Southey read it because of him. Shelley never lost his love of it. De Quincey, at Oxford, proudly thought himself its only reader.[20] And Charles Lamb, with his incomparable flair for literature, in a letter in 1799, to Southey, puns on "gibberish"; then he adds, "But Gebor hath some lucid intervals. I remember darkly one beautiful simile veiled in uncouth phrases about the youngest daughter of the Ark." [21] The passage is a rather Miltonic one, part of a description of Charoba hoping for signs of life in Gebir:

> Never so eager, when the world was waves,
> Stood the less daughter of the ark, and tried
> (Innocent this temptation!) to recall
> With folded vest, and casting arm, the dove.[22]

In 1824, Lamb quotes to Thomas Hood, without giving the source, and in as casually allusive a way as if the lines were Shakespeare:

"He sang in meads how sweet the brooklets ran,/To the rough ocean and red restless sands." [23] The actual words, in Book IV, constitute a song, or enough of one to give us a sense of completeness: "In smiling meads how sweet the brooks repose,/To the rough ocean and red restless sands!" Lamb's unconscious invention is pleasant enough: "smiling" is no loss, though the last half of Landor's line deserves to be restored—for itself and for the sentence as a whole. But there is rightly no mistake about the next line. A third party may be allowed to compliment Landor and Lamb for their behavior at the two ends of the art of verbal communication.

Without a lively feeling for words there is no literature; compared with it, the questions of technique that absorb the critic, and the forms of literature, and form itself, beyond the sentence, are a supererogation, a lure, a vanity, or a mere convenience. But, if literature is made, it needs to be heard; and without convenience and attraction in terms of form there may be no hearers. Not to exaggerate the weakness of *Gebir* as a unit, a piece of architecture, or a machine, it has nevertheless always been read, when it has been read at all, not for itself but for things that are in it. *Mutatis mutandis,* the same could be said of *Hamlet.*

Those few hungerers after literature must have found in *Gebir* an intensity of color, of chiaroscuro, of image, and of movement that was still but newly returning to Europe. There is in it such appreciation of dramatic gesture as in these lines: "Then with a long and tacit step, one arm/Behind, and every finger wide outspread,/He look'd and totter'd on a black abyss." [24] The poet has, to the finger-tips, felt his body in the place. And there are other romantic thrills in a more or less Classical underworld: "he turn'd —/And stood held breathless in a ghost's embrace." [25] But that is for the children. Gebir is appalled to learn that in that inhuman place " 'Justice is supreme;/Compassion can be but where passions are.' " [26] The thought, like any other good one, drops from a nerve end.

Some of the attractions of *Gebir* do little more than ride the senses:

> I still hear shrieking, through the moonless night,
> Their discontented and deserted shades.[27]

> When at their incantation would the Moon
> Start back, and shuddering shed blue blasted light.[28]

or

> And now the gulph divides us, and the waves
> Of sulphur bellow through the blue abyss.[29]

"Bellow through the blue abyss" is fun, but it inclines the ear away from this planet, away from true imagination, born of experience, which, on the one hand, enables us "To drive the dolphins from the wreathed door" [30] (is the enchantment of that line not only in the sounds, but in the suggestion of wreathed and watery movement and the immemorial love of men and dolphins?)—and, on the other hand, simply grants us the quiet happiness of recognition, to know, in our own feet, that someone else's "not firm'd,/Slipt backward from the wither'd grass short-graz'd." [31]

What could be more commonplace? We can imagine a poem on "The Art of Walking Uphill," in which we would expect innumerable details in evidence of the author's close observation of his feet and what they trod on; in such a poem, the leaping to life of something caught in the corner of his attention—something vividly true about a lizard, a bird, a flower, a rock under the hand —would be a refreshment and an assurance of the author's worth as a companion. So in hearing, in *Gebir,* these few words about the grass, we may be drawn alert and smiling, pleased that the author had with such almost unnecessary but rewarding care imagined himself in the place. "Now how did he think of that?" is the natural question. "That is exactly what might have happened." This recognition comes as a satisfying surprise, particularly in a poem whose subject matter is the reverse of the commonplace; and part of the satisfaction is in the way it suddenly raises the backdrop on the scene of common life, pastoral in truth, across which the extraordinary must always flicker its story, like shadows of clouds against the solid hills.

The words themselves (apart from the observation) of the poet did not detain us longer than if they had been not verse but plain explanatory prose. Somewhere else along the scale of knowledge, in a place where the registered fact begins to swell into meditation and music, comes this passage about Queen Charoba in her grief:

> The turban that betray'd its golden charge
> Within, the veil that down her shoulders hung,
> All fallen at her feet! the furthest wave
> Creeping with silent progress up the sand,
> Glided thro' all, and rais'd their hollow folds.[32]

Rarest of all are the two best-known passages from the poem: that lovely voluntary that goes

> But I have sinuous shells, of pearly hue
> Within, and they that lustre have imbibed
> In the sun's palace porch; where, when unyoked,
> His chariot wheel stands midway in the wave.
> Shake one, and it awakens; then apply
> Its polished lips to your attentive ear,
> And it remembers its august abodes,
> And murmurs as the ocean murmurs there.[33]

And that magnificent image, introduced by a night-long mile of monosyllable: "And the long moon-beam on the hard wet sand/ Lay like a jaspar column half uprear'd." [34] Not all beauty takes the breath away; this does.

Consummate poetry is not liberated from common life, but out of common life it makes something new of words locked together in so foredoomed a way that they will not budge. Such poetry is rare in any body of work. Meanwhile it is a happy thing for a listener, enjoying the sound of his author's words, to say to himself, "He too has been there." This can often be said of Landor as early as *Gebir,* which he may have written when he was twenty.

IV   The Larger-than-life: Tragedy.
Count Julian.

In February, 1811, Landor wrote to Southey of *Count Julian,* which he was still correcting, "I finished this tragedy only because I thought it disgraceful to have formed so many plans and to have completed none. Indeed, I had some doubt whether I could write a tragedy, a thing which I have always considered as a *desideratum* in modern literature." [35] We may discount the implication of a mere act of will, without underestimating the part played in an artist's life by the need to exercise, to stretch, his talents. This piece he had taken particular trouble to construct well: "The plan and characters are well proportioned, which is sure to please people, though they know not why. The events of the first act lead naturally to the last, and every scene is instrumental to the catastrophe." [36] Knowing little about the theater, Landor would have liked to see it staged, and yet his pride would not run the risk of its being refused by John Kemble; but, when the publisher

Longman refused to print it, even at Landor's expense, Landor spoke of his literary career as a thing of the past and burned the manuscript of another tragedy, *Ferrante and Giulio.* Vigorous as well as mercurial, Landor recovered—as he was to do from disappointments greater than this one during the long course of his life.

Count Julian, which was published by John Murray a year later, is the story of a Spanish conqueror who, to avenge the rape of his daughter by his king, led back into his country the Moors he had just before driven out. The Spanish subject was a sympathetic one to Landor, for he had been soldiering in Spain only two years before. As a tender man who could bear no affront, and as one already familiar with the pain of anger and the loneliness of whole-souled individuality, he might be expected to penetrate the character of Count Julian and the tragedy he lived and caused.

To De Quincey, Landor had certainly done so: "Mr. Landor, who always rises with his subject, and dilates like Satan into Teneriffe or Atlas, when he sees before him an antagonist worthy of his powers, is probably the one man in Europe that has adequately conceived the situation, the stern self-dependency and the monumental misery of Count Julian." [37] De Quincey, not certain that he has quite conveyed his impression, goes on: ". . . after all has been done which intellectual power *could* do since Aeschylus (and since Milton in his Satan), no embodiment of the Promethean situation, none of the Promethean character, fixes the attentive eye upon itself with the same secret feeling of fidelity to the vast archetype, as Mr. Landor's 'Count Julian.' " [38]

Long afterward, Swinburne, in his article on Landor in the ninth edition of the *Encyclopaedia Britannica,* called *Count Julian* "the sublimest poem published in our language between the last masterpiece of Milton and the first masterpiece of Shelley." [39] The persistence of such excitement tells us something of what Landor's early exercises in grandeur could mean to men of his time, born in the blandness of the eighteenth century. A twentieth-century reader accustomed first to the heights and latterly to the depths of Romanticism may grant at least that, in his fall, Julian suffers no lapse in dignity. There are, as we have already come to expect, memorably impressive passages—one even in revelation of his weakness:

> The hand that hurled thy chariot o'er its wheels,
> That held thy steeds erect and motionless

> As moulten statues on some palace-gates,
> Shakes, as with palsied age, before thee now.[40]

Southey called this "the grandest image of power that ever poet produced." [41] A reader might wish away "palsied age," but the "steeds erect" in that imperial grasp are not to be quibbled at. Another image that has been called sublime is that of the eagle, and of Julian in heroic isolation:

> Wakeful he sits, and lonely, and unmoved,
> Beyond the arrows, views, or shouts of men;
> As oftentimes an eagle, when the sun
> Throws o'er the varying earth his early rays,
> Stands solitary, stands immovable
> Upon some highest cliff, and rolls his eye,
> Clear, constant, unobservant, unabased,
> In the cold light, above the dews of morn.[42]

On the elevated level there is little more to be found. At the very end of Act III, Julian addresses Roderigo, who has been whining for forgiveness.

> I do conjure thee; raise not in my soul
> Again the tempest that has wrecked my fame;
> Thou shalt not breathe in the same clime with her.
> Far o'er the unebbing sea thou shalt adore
> The eastern star, and—may thy end be peace.

That internal tempest takes one back to Achilles, leaping from the embrace of grief and charity in which he and Priam had been held; but in these lines of Landor there is no Nature and no Homer; indeed, nobody is talking to anybody.

The impression that Landor is engaged in a rhetorical exercise is heightened by the respectable monotony of his blank verse:

> *Covilla.* And war, in all its fury, roams o'er Spain!
> *Julian.* Alas! and will for ages: crimes are loose
> At which ensanguined War stands shuddering;
> And calls for vengeance from the powers above,
> Impatient of inflicting it himself.
> Nature, in these new horrors, is aghast
> At her own progeny, and knows them not.
> I am the minister of wrath; the hands
> That tremble at me, shall applaud me too,
> And seal their condemnation.[43]

Having to write a tragedy for some hungry actors might encourage a poet to think of human beings. Landor is thinking only of writing a tragedy; he has in mind heroic characters and events, and all in heroic verse that must not get out of hand. "I sometimes rise into too high a key," he told Southey in November, 1810; "but I have an instinctive horror of declamation." [44] The self-criticism is precise; and the preciseness and the self-consciousness keep a man well back from that abyss whose rim is the playground of tragedy and epic. Landor will have to feel his way to where he is at home.

Count Julian is, then, blank verse in a certain posture, not words alive with character and idea. The dialogue is a string of solo recitations, not true soliloquies and not arias but speeches emitted from the front of the mouth in the direction of an audience. In *Gebir* as well, there was no sense of confrontation of character with character, but none was particularly needed; and after all there was Dalica, who, while presumably addressing her sister, and only presumably, was yet really talking, colorfully—to herself.

Now and then a little life gets into the dialogue of *Count Julian,* when self-hood is realized in words—literally so in the twenty-seventh line of Act III, where one reader's pleasure is interrupted by good drama that is not Landor's. Opas asks Roderigo what, after such losses, remains to him; and the answer comes, "Myself —Roderigo—/Whom hatred cannot reach, nor love cast down." When to the question of Nérine—*"Dans un si grand revers, que vous reste-t-il"*—Corneille's Médée, ending the verse, so famously replied, *"Moi,"* [45] Corneille could be complimented on his fine adaptation of the *"Medea superest"* of Seneca. But there is no reason for Landor's borrowing, and it cheapens his play. Perhaps Landor thought he was the first discoverer of this reply; for, of all writers, there has been none less willing to be beholden to others for his mind's work. Or perhaps the best comment might be a maxim of Chamfort: *"On a trouvé le moi de Médée sublime; mais celui qui ne peut pas le dire dans tous les accidents de la vie est bien peu de chose, ou plutôt n'est rien."* [46]

Life gets into the play—into its words—when the poet is actively concerned with it. Reputation, tragedy, grandeur, style, are, as subjects of contemplation, not so likely to give birth as is something less abstract that, by teasing the sympathies, wins and wakes the mind. There is a good deal of eloquence in the following, but the poet has only achieved a posture.

> Already I behold my funeral.
> The turbid cities wave and swell with it,
> And wrongs are lost in that day's pageantry:
> Opprest and desolate, the countryman
> Receives it like a gift; he hastens home,
> Shews where the hoof of Moorish horse laid waste
> His narrow croft and winter garden-plot,
> Sweetens with fallen pride his children's lore,
> And points their hatred; but applauds their tears.[47]

The words do not give substance to Julian, who speaks them; they might as well come from a chorus. Equally alive as words, equally choric, but very different in their source and their effect, are these of Hernando:

> Who that beheld our sails from off the hights,
> Like the white birds, nor larger, tempt the gale
> In sunshine and in shade, now almost touch
> The solitary shore, glance, turn, retire,
> Would think these lovely playmates could portend
> Such mischief to the world; such blood, such woe;
> Could draw to them from far the peaceful hinds,
> Cull the gay flower of cities, and divide
> Friends, children, every bond of human life;
> Could dissipate whole families, could sink
> Whole states in ruin, at one hour, one blow.[48]

Where is monotony now? Where strain or artifice? The poet is not trying to be or trying to do; he *is:* in lilting mastery he is thinking.

V *A Grandeur within Our Reach:* Andrea of Hungary

On the elevated level, a writer cannot be friends with his characters, hate their enemies, enjoy their mannerisms, their tastes in food, their politics, and watch how wise, how noble a mere man or woman may be; in fact, on the elevated level a writer cannot be his own main character. A Landor cannot breathe up there, but all levels are comfortable to a Shakespeare, whose own self appears to have been less interesting to him than that of anyone who happened to appear in his cast of characters; in discarding himself,

Shakespeare could be anybody. To discard himself is the last thing that Walter Savage Landor would have found it possible or even remotely desirable to do. His writing was an assertion of himself. He was a self-conscious man and a conscious artist, and he could not think in terms of the high-tragical drama, charged with its cosmic anonymity.

A perfectionist in language, Landor was limited by temperament and by life itself to what may more or less be perfected, but the winds of the universe are not in this category. Tragedy itself he might try to write by paying his respects to its convention of high levels and superior beings—and by keeping his distance, by guarding the work from the impertinence of his own personality. We have seen in *Count Julian,* however, that when Landor relaxed his grim-lipped effort to be tremendous and, looking at the earth, gave his vocabulary its freedom, the result was a moment of poetry and life. When he was the natural Landor, the never nameless participant in life, the drama came alive on his own level, as pathos, as melodrama, as romance.

Releasing himself from any need to imitate conquerors or to think himself into heroic proportions, Landor found room to exercise his poetic ambition on another plane—among a multitude of splendors and miseries, historic and nearly so, measured in terms of intensity rather than altitude, where heroism is possible because there are tyrants. It is a world for which human beings are responsible, one in which character rules; it is a moral, social, political world which excites our pity and our terror; but it is not the world of tragedy. It arouses our affections, as well, and laughter and indignation. The intimate tone of it permits the poet to draw his characters at length, even at the expense of plot; in this romantic quest of the personal, the trappings of majesty do not hold us off but allure us.

"In the characters generally," said Landor in a letter received by Forster on November 2, 1838, "I have avoided strong contrasts. These are the certain signs of a weak artist." [49] He was speaking of *Andrea of Hungary,* the first play in his trilogy that freely treats the story of Giovanna of Naples; and this trilogy caused Julius Hare to tell Landor that the life of tragedy in England was in the hands of Landor, Henry Taylor, and George Darley. [50] In the first play, young Andrea, just married to the even younger Giovanna, Queen

of Naples, is murdered, by exactly whose hands we are not certain;
but we do know that the instigator was Fra Rupert, his tutor and
guardian, who has limitless political and personal ambitions.

In the second play, *Giovanna of Naples,* Giovanna, cleared of
guilt, marries her beloved cousin Luigi of Taranto; in the third,
Fra Rupert, Giovanna, now married to Duke Otho of Brunswick,
is dethroned by Charles of Durazzo, her nephew whom she has
reared as a son; and she is murdered in imprisonment. Fra Rupert,
the villain of villains, stabs himself. The whole story is about the
powerful, distributing and redistributing power, and about a few
sympathetic victims of the process. Nothing could be more crudely
machined than the machinations themselves; they are there because
they somehow must be: patent lies are swallowed with enthusiasm,
impossible deals are made, heavy-footed agents slink noisily off
into the night. And Landor shows no mastery of dramatic timing
and proportion. Something has happened to somebody on the
balcony: here is Andrea's cap—down falls the Queen; here is his
cloak with a spot of blood on it—down falls the final curtain.
"My scenes fall in the natural order," Landor explains. "What is
plot but *trick?*" [51] Two months later, on Christmas Day, 1838,
Landor wrote to G. P. R. James: "In my opinion, neither of my
Dramas [*Andrea* and *Giovanna*] will do very well for the stage.
There is little plot—in other words, little trick and perplexity.
I do not find them among the ancient Greeks—I find strait and
simple folds, and no knots." [52] This view of the place of plot in
literature is worth taking seriously, but not in the present case,
in which it is vitiated, or at least troubled, by what seems to be
Landor's incapacity. What he is truly interested in is character,
and the revisions and additions sent to Forster show it—character
in verse, opening up to us glimpses of what are in life its variety
and iridescence.

The charm of Andrea is unlooked for, a gift for us from the
generous mind of Landor. To draw our sympathies, the nineteen-
year-old boy need only have been good, gentle, and brave; he is,
instead, a whole and unique invention—as we begin to see at the
very opening of the play:

> What say you now, Giovanna! shall we go
> And conquer France? Heigho! I am sadly idle;
> My mighty mind wants full activity.

But the motherly Giovanna, two years younger, cannot joke about such dread matters: 'Andrea! be contented; stay at home;/Conquer? you've conquer'd me.' She is no fribble. "I have sworn to love him," she tells her sister Maria; and, when Maria exclaims "What a vow!," Giovanna answers: "The harder to perform/The greater were the glory: I will earn it." [53] Wisely she fixes upon the good she sees in him beneath the ignorance (Fra Rupert has deprived him of education in order to maintain control of him), the unpolished manners, the apparent irresponsibility, and the lazy oblivion to political jealousies and snares.

The characters of Giovanna and Andrea unfold before us as she, speaking to Filippa, analyzes his:

> Sterile the soil is not! hard! hard! 'tis waste.
> What buoyant spirits and what pliant temper!
> How patient of reproof! how he wipes off
> All injuries before they harden on him,
> And wonders at affronts, and doubts they can be!
> Then, his wild quickness! O the churl that bent it
> Into the earth, colourless, shapeless, thriftless,
> Fruitless, for ever! Had he been my brother,
> I should have wept all my life over him;
> But, being my husband, one hypocrisy
> I must put on, one only ever will I.
> Others must think, by my observance of him,
> I hold him prudent, penetrating, firm,
> No less than virtuous. . . .[54]

A moment later she refers to his "Wit of bright feather, but of broken wing." The great test of any writer capable of crediting a character with such traits and with "his wild quickness" is to show them in action. Landor not only passed this test but did more: he made of Andrea something that, as in life itself, we may almost know; and then the contours fade off into wonder.

We know Andrea for a day, and he develops rapidly, like some rare flower. He is already in fatal rebellion against Fra Rupert when we first see them together, and he is much too candid and free. After he has told Rupert he loathes him, he grows more and more alert, as if conscious of being invisibly surrounded; his eyes and his mind dart into and out of corners. But his heart opens itself to be that of a husband and lover:

> But thou too ridest like a queen, my dove!
> *Giovanna.* So very like one? Would you make me proud?
> *Andrea.* God forbid that! I love thee more for beauty.

> Ne'er put on pride, my heart! thou dost not want it;
> Many there are who do; cast it to them
> Who cannot do without it, empty souls!
> Ha! how you look! is it surprise or pleasure? [55]

Though he can still trifle, he does so absent-mindedly, as one entertaining the children:

> *Maria, coaxing.* No, no; you won't be angry, prince!
> *Andrea.* I said
> Half-angry, and resolve to keep my word.
> *Maria.* Anger is better as pomegranates are,
> Split into halves, and losing no small part.
> *Andrea.* I never heard such truth about pomegranates!
> What was the other thing we reason'd on?
> Ho! now I recollect, as you shall see. [*Goes: all follow.*] [56]

When he learns that two young nobles named Caraffa and Caraccioli have been strangled (does he suspect Rupert? Uncertainty plays a large part in this dusky tale), he recalls that one of them had disliked him for no reason that he knew. And in a moment, though with the humor of embarrassment he gives his feelings a cuff, he breaks into half-hysterical tears:

> Without a word of hearing, he is gone!
> To think of this! to think how he has fallen
> Amid his pranks and joyances, amid
> His wild heath myrtle-blossoms, one might say,
> It quite unmans me. [57]

That "one might say," in its measured humorous restraint, meant to shrug off the exquisite expression that precedes it—that alone could win for Landor the title of dramatist. A reader may also notice the breathlessness, the wide gesturing, in the placement of the word "amid." This is a burdened Andrea, nearing the end of a day that he began with such appetite and such vivid responses as in these words:

> Rather should you have heard, as there you might,
> Quarrelsome blunder-headed drums, o'erpowered
> By pelting cymbals; then complaining flutes,
> And boy-voiced fifes, lively, and smart, and shrill;
> Then timbrels, where tall fingers trip, but trip
> In the right place, and run along again;
> Then blustering trumpets, wonder-wafting horns,

> *Evvivas* from their folks, *hurrahs* from ours,
> And songs that pour into both ears long life
> And floods of glory and victory for ever— [58]

He enters the evening of it in this fashion:

Andrea. Keep back: where thieves may be, leave men alone.
Now for drawn swords! Where are they; slipt behind
The mulberry: wisely schemed! 'twon't do! come forth!
Yield! tremble like a poplar-leaf! Who art thou?
[*Seizing* Boccaccio.]
Boccaccio. King Robert, sir, respected me.
Andrea. Did *he?*
Did *he?* Then far more highly should Andrea.
Sicily! treat him kindly. We may all,
Even you and I, commit an indiscretion.
How the stars twinkle! how the light leaves titter!
And there are secret quiverings in the herbs,
As if they all knew something of the matter,
And wisht it undisturb'd. To-night no harm
Shall happen to the worst man in Aversa.[59]

The quality of his speech ripens, and saddens, and refines as it
grows toward valediction:

> We have not spoken more to-day, my chuck,
> Than many other days, yet thou appearest
> Wiser than ever. I have gain'd from thee
> More than I gave.[60]

Whatever criticisms remain to be spoken, we may now understand
what Browning meant when he dedicated the eighth volume of
Bells and Pomegranates to Landor, "a Great Dramatic Poet."

It would be hard to imagine anyone's reading *Andrea of
Hungary* and not *Giovanna of Naples* and *Fra Rupert.* One at
least wants to have survived all those dangers oneself. And there
are numerous interesting people along the way. Even the conspira-
tors are not all alike. We meet a famous figure, Rienzi, in a scene
in which his wife tries to keep him good though great. Besides
these pleasures, there is the fact that no experience of the trilogy
is complete until Fra Rupert has been disposed of. But, of this
most substantial of Landor's dramatic works, the best part is the
first, the play of Andrea.

Giovanna's play is as curiously incomplete as Andrea's: the
curtain decapitates the eager spectator. Giovanna herself, bereft

of Andrea, does not become anything but highly admirable. A moment of humor gives an illusion that we have seen another aspect of her; it turns out, however, to have been not so much Giovanna as generic woman, as when she makes hectic but useless attempts to conceal from an old knight her concern for Luigi in battle outside the walls. Beside herself, she, at last, in relief, whispers in soliloquy: "Praises to thee, O Virgin! who concealedst/ So kindly all my fondness, half my fears!" [61] Giovanna, though not so interesting as the hard-bitten and faithful Filippa, her foster-mother, or even as her sister Maria, is a noble woman. The last thing she does is to refuse to abdicate. "Farewell then! You may live and serve your country;/These walls are mine, and nothing now beyond." [62]

To Landor, the subject of this whole chain of events is the inhumanity of ambition, the cruelty of authoritarian power. "Ambition," says Rienzi's wife, "is but Avarice in mail,/Blinder, and often weaker." [63] The agony caused by this force, and the murders, cannot even by the reader be shaken off. Once in a while, someone is sorry, as is the conspirator Maximin—or Margarita, the wife of Charles of Durazzo, when she remembers at last how Giovanna, Charles's prisoner, had cherished them when they were children:

> *Margarita.* O Carlo! O my Carlo!
> I have . . . (will God forgive me?) been ungrateful.
> And all this time! . . when but one moment of it . . .
> My hand in her's, or her's upon my head . . .
> *Durazzo.* Hush! Margarita! thou'art a queen: be calm,
> And worthy of the station we enjoy.[64]

Landor must have been intensely happy while at work on Rupert; and so perfectly successful is this figure in his unconscionable melodramatic villainy that only an unimaginative spoilsport could laugh him off, or could not wish to see him writhing for a long while on the rack. In the end, he says to himself that he has been rent on the rack of conscience. He is more convincing in his grand metaphor of the great man as an Antaeus whose foot must press the people:

> Away from court?
> No; never. Leave the people? When he leaves it,
> The giant is uplifted off the earth
> And loses all his strength. My foot must press it.[65]

This beast dies with dignity.

The trilogy ends with the wailing of the populace for Giovanna murdered:

> *Second Officer.* Their queen's name they cry . . .
> *Third Officer.* With blessings.
> *First Officer.* Now, at last, ye know Giovanna;
> And now will Rupert too be known, tho' late.

The sense of waste is heavy. Our feelings have been engaged throughout, and our poet has, as if speaking for history, refused to tend our wounds. The events are terrible and pitiful, and the secret of *katharsis* has escaped him, as it has how many others of less than his purity of intent. That secret—is it known to any, save by dumb wisdom or instinct, that path to "calm of mind, all passion spent"?

VI   The Siege of Ancona

The only other drama Landor completed is *The Siege of Ancona,* written in October, 1844. Landor was nearly seventy, and the play is warm with his feelings. Oliver Elton said that in it "action and style are as clear as they are heroic. It is perhaps the most faultless of his longer poems." [66] I agree with Sidney Colvin, but without his judicious hesitation when he writes that "the play, although the least noticed by his critics, is I think, upon the whole, his best." [67] The clarity mentioned by Elton is most noticeable; the play flows with an ease of natural expression rare in blank verse or in any other kind. We shift from one set of important characters to another in such a way that suspense is continued action, and the change of scene contributes to the uninterrupted unfolding of the whole.

The Archbishop of Mentz, who is leading the forces of Barbarossa against the town of Ancona, requires only that the citizens relinquish their "lawless independence" and submit. The Consul refuses to consider this demand; and, until the siege is lifted by kind neighbors, the people of Ancona, both men and women, fight gloriously against starvation and the foe. All the forces of this drama are before us, in the open, on the faces and tongues of the characters; nothing in it is mysterious, and nothing more subtle than aggression and defense, independence, ingenuity, love, loyalty, and modest heroism. The Pope has offered to help Ancona if the Consul will accept the Pope's nephew as his son-in-law; Erminia, in every way the Consul's daughter, scorns the temptation and the papal wiles. Erminia's is the other side of the story; for the shy, sweet, angry, and unspoken love of Erminia and Stamura is not a subplot. After we realize that Ancona will be saved, these two lovers are all we care about; although we like, respect, even revere almost everybody, all that remains is to see the manner in which one young pair of eyes meets another. What critics have neglected to observe about *The Siege of Ancona* is that it is a romance— and a very satisfactory one.

The play begins with our seeing through the young Erminia's eyes the great procession of the archbishop marching against the city. It ends with Erminia and Stamura, two in the midst of a great ceremonial company, after a touch of romantic comedy. If we have not known that Stamura's mind has wandered, we are economically informed of it:

> *Countess.* There is a sword here bright enough to throw
> A lustre on Stamura. Marchesella!
> *Marchesella.* Kneel, sir! [*He kneels to* ERMINIA.]
> *Countess.* Not there.
> *Marchesella.* Yes, there; what fitter place?

Although our two young people play very important roles in the siege, and although the "other side of the story" was laid down with care in advance, neither these two nor any individual is allowed to seem more important than the siege itself and the suffering of the people. This effect is not the result of tact alone; the author was guided by instinctive sensitivity to values:

> *Consul.* We some are poor, we some are prosperous,
> We all alike owe all we have: the air
> Is life alike to all, the sun is warmth,
> The earth, its fruits and flocks, are nutriment,
> Children and wives are comforts; all partake
> (Or may partake) in these. Shall hoarded grain
> Or gold be less in common, when the arms
> That guard it are not those that piled it up,
> But those that shrink without it? Come, ye rich,
> Be richer still: strengthen your brave defenders,
> And make all yours that was not yours before.
> Dares one be affluent where ten thousand starve?
> Open your treasuries, your granaries,
> But throw mine open first.[68]

These lines contain the deeper notes that Landor heard within his subject and that caused him to choose to write the play in the first place. There was a great opportunity for eloquence against the history of the church, but Landor rejected it. The story is a heroic one, and the springs of it are nothing so shallow as persons and institutions; they are human vices and virtues. The Archbishop, for instance, is made to tell the Consul that anyone who minds Holy Writ will mind the plainest part of it and the part most worth remembering: "Render unto Caesar the things that are Caesar's." This opinion is momentarily amusing in itself, as well as here in the midst of a sermon which the Consul is delivering to him on pride. The Archbishop is not allowed to look ridiculous, however; for the Consul's bitter summary of what men owe to Caesar is coolly added to by the Archbishop: "We shall want more by Sunday."

> *Consul.* May the curse
> Of God be on you!
> *Archbishop.* We are not so impious:
> It *is* on you: it were a sin to wish it.[69]

What has happened here is that Landor's mind has transcended all individual reference—transcended even satire. It would be difficult to find a fuller and more powerfully condensed presentation of the whole story of man in society—of humanity on one hand and of all that is meant by "Caesar" on the other. The two figures march unbent, not only through the play, but over the horizon of any imaginable future.

A simpler passage-at-arms is that between the heroic and ingenious Father John (who must make weight against some less worthy men of God in Landor's work) and the Bishop of Ancona.[70] Father John is a normal character; the Bishop, a comic one. Though he fails to respond to Father John's call for an ounce of flour to save a mother and child, it would not be easy to hate him: he is not real enough; and, even in comic terms, he is more mad than vicious. Incidentally, Father John makes, in asides, two rather good jokes in this scene; no doubt the fact ought to be remembered when the question of Landor's humor is raised. But if the scene were dropped from the play, it would not be missed; it is not serious enough, and it is not so true as the romance.

VII   *More People in Plays*

It was for Landor a pleasant occupation to write fragmentary dramas—sketches and scenes—in verse. "Ines de Castro" is as long as most; and, like the others, it was not, I think, done for the sake of poetry but to arouse our sympathy and admiration for one character and our hatred and admiration for another. The sketches that Stephen Wheeler groups under "Scenes Greek and Roman" are an exception; for these are dramatic poems rather than dramas: imaginary conversations in verse.

In 1828, Landor had published a short imaginary conversation in prose called "Ines de Castro at Cintra"; it falls into blank verse, only some of which is acknowledged by being set up as such. This fault of taste and craftsmanship is a rarity in Landor. The whole was gradually turned into verse and enlarged into the series of dramatic scenes that were published in the 1846 edition of his works. Particularly interesting is a footnote to the original, in which he says of Camoëns' treament of Ines in the *Lusiads* that "This distinguished and admirable poet was not felicitous in the development of character; which, whatever may be talked of and repeated on the beautiful and the sublime, is the best and most arduous part of poetry. It is this which gives to Homer a large portion of his glory; it is this which sustains us half-stifled in the Socratic school of Euripides; and it is this which, even with a third of the poetry, would have elevated Shakespeare immeasurably above all." [71] So long as he retained in his mind the importance of this principle, and so long as he continued to have literary ambitions, Landor could not have been content to be either an essayist or a lyric poet.

At the beginning of "Ines de Castro," we are informed that "the events in these scenes are not strictly historical." Landor is not interested in chronology, or in whether or not the King or the Queen had Ines put to death; his interest is character—the faithful love between Prince Pedro of Portugal and his mistress Ines de Castro, their marriage after the death of his wife, and the eventual success of the Queen his mother in doing away with his lovely, uncommon commoner. The three main characters are briefly delineated in the following three sentences:

> *Pedro.* Merciless queen, abstain!
> *Ines.* O call none merciless! all *must* have mercy;
> All need it.

> *Queen.* Hold thy peace! art thou in church,
> Profane one! or are words like these for thee! [72]

The Queen is not fond of cant, though, like all intolerable
women, she sees herself as one who has much to bear: "Long-
suffering is my merit, if the grace/Of God vouchsafes me one.
. . ." [73] That touch of modesty is all to the good in the portrait of
a woman who calls in the assassins; so also is a rasp of humor
in the scene in which she poisons the mind of her silly, doddering
royal husband: "*Alfonso.* I have been younger./*Blanca.* Chroniclers
may assert it." [74] Her words at the end, while looking at the corpse
of Ines, are not so good: "The scene quite saddens me./'Twas
her own fault, rash child! God's will be done!" The perfection of
her moral blindness, though required for the satire, is too much,
too precisely as we would have it; moreover, she has been too
intelligent to think in this way. Yet Ines was indeed a rash child,
and that the Queen's hatred is so powerful it blinds the hater is
brilliantly indicated in such energetic lines as

> Ay, sob!
> Hide thy white face! pull thy loose curls around,
> Exactly like . . . I know not what they're like,
> They are so frightful . . . tossing here and there
> By their own rustic untamed springiness. . . .[75]

Don Pedro must be too many things to be quite clearly a self:
a kind adulterer, a vigorous partisan of his mistress, a legitimizer
of his bastards, an anticlerical liberal, and a rather helpless man;
he is busy enough talking, and opposing his mother, but, though
appealing, he remains amorphous. To say that Queen Blanca is
the character most vividly drawn is only to say that evil has more
substance than good. Ines, though she cannot be allowed to do
anything but suffer, has been dowered with an unusually sweet
and generous simplicity. She responds quickly, blithely, tenderly
to everything about her, and deeply to what comes from the heart;
like a musical instrument, she holds back nothing for herself but
exists in giving. Only quotation at considerable length could
illustrate her and the way she throbs in the air of these scenes,
like certain of the notes of a song.

Of Landor's other women characters at least one, Anne Boleyn,
has a somewhat comparable charming sweetness. Presented to us
only in one scene of no more than a hundred and six lines, her
character is depicted in her conversation with the Constable of

the Tower of London. That character is flawlessly beautiful, and
she is believable because each of us has known one or two persons
who thought less of themselves than of others. Such a recognition
is, however, only the first step toward an understanding between
author and reader; Landor must carry us beyond it. For one thing,
he presents us with an unsuspected side of Anne's life; it is made
clear that she was constantly receiving from her subjects individual
requests for help, for she breaks the Constable's heart by assuming
that the Writ of Execution he must ask her to read is "A helpless
widow's innocent petition" and by asking him to take it back
since she is no queen and has no almoner.[76] We learn during this
speech, while she enlarges on her inability to do anything now
for poor widows, that Anne is capable of a merely feminine self-
pity: "Ignorant are you, or incredulous,/That not a clasp is left
me? not a stone/The vilest. . . ." [77] But it comes only as a flash
of her general awareness, feminine certainly, sinks into the
motherhood of her thoughts for Elizabeth, "whose cradle/Rocks
in my ear and almost crazes me," [78] and helps to make real her
conquest of tragedy. Her one allusion to anything that might be
termed religious faith is an appreciation of this world that is
deeply human, pagan, and womanly. She has been recalling her
pleasure in her baby:

> *Constable.* Oh, spare those words!
> *Anne.* Why spare them? when I feel
> Departure from this world would never be
> Departure from its joys: the joys of heaven
> Would mingle with them scarcely with fresh sweetness.[79]

The last four words are inharmonious, but they show knowledge
of life.

There are other instances in which Landor has made the
dramatic essence of an episode almost palpable and yet failed to
write memorably. "Walter Tyrrel and William Rufus" is a piece
of perfect romantic characterization; not only are we there on
horseback between Rufus, a live, heavily breathing tyrant, and
Tyrrel, a live, sensitive, and brave gentleman who dares to kill
him; but our hearts are in it, and we must love Tyrrel and hate
Rufus. The language communicates by jostling us.

> *Bishop.* God's blood! were I no bishop . . .
> *Tyrrel.* Then thy own
> Were cooler.

> *Bishop.* Whip that hound aside! O Christ!
> The beast has paw'd my housings! What a day
> For dirt!
> *Tyrrel.* The scent lies well; pity no more
> The housings; look, my lord! here trots the King! [80]

A writer cannot expect shouting and profanity to do all his en-
livening for him; more than may be immediately noticeable is
done here by the specific and rousing "paw'd" and "trots," and
by the ironic abruptness of "pity."

Landor plays fair in his portrayal of Rufus. A lesser artist might
have piled fictional on historical abomination and have ended with
a storybook monster; though Landor's Rufus is bad enough to be
recognizable, yet he is oddly rather a good sort for an unconscionable villain. And he speaks as well as anybody in the scene:

> Tyrrel! thou didst right
> And dutifully, to remove the house
> Of thy forefathers. 'Twas an odd request,
> To leave the dovecote, for the sake of those
> Flea-bitten blind old pigeons. [81]

And Tyrrel is as true a man as any in fiction. The little work
is a vivid experience of oppression, manliness, humaneness, and
poetic sensibility that remains with us; the communication seems
complete—only, vivid though the language is, the words do not
linger in the ear or call us back to themselves. Landor's passionate
concern with the subject carries it; but the language, having served
its purpose, has gone off into the air forgotten. It was all that
language need be, except for something memorable that would
have preserved it.

There was no reason why Landor should not have gone on
writing more and more such sketches in verse, and he did continue
to write dramatic verse as the years went on. In fact, late in 1855
he was working on "Antony and Octavius: Scenes for the Study,"
which he finished in January, 1856. The dedication shows how
conscious he is of writing in an "old-fashioned and obsolete" style
of composition, and the preface indicates how much it is the work
of a reader, loitering, as he says, in the paths of "Shakespeare's
garden." But "Antony and Octavius" has its own virtue, and much
of it lies in the strength and consistency of Landor's modeling of
Octavius, the great man, the mortal god, and the destroyer of

children in his insatiable lust for security. In Scene 12, proof enough of the continuance of the poet's powers into his eighties, Octavia pleads the human cause against her brother's assertion of his own:

> *Octavius.* Are children always children?
> *Octavia.* O brother! brother! are men always men?
> They are full-grown then only when grown up
> Above their fears. Power never yet stood safe;
> Compass it round with friends and kindnesses,
> And not with moats of blood. Remember Thebes. . . .

To her examples, he replies, "Thou art not yet, Octavia, an old woman;/Tell not, I do beseech thee, such old tales." [82] The piece ends with Octavia; she speaks for the poet, and his comment may be reduced to two of her lines: "I lack not wisdom utterly; my soul/Assures me wisdom is humanity." [83]

Alert, pragmatic, bitingly cold, Octavius rules the work; Antony, Cleopatra, and even Agrippa, against whose kindness the outlines of Octavius are cruelly etched, pale and disappear from mind before the last word is reached. Something, however, outlasts even Octavius in the mind of the reader, and that is words more stout than those of which he is made—these, for instance, making Maecenas's comment on hatred—"It is too troublesome; it rumples sleep,/It settles on the dishes of the feast,/It bites the fruit, it dips into the wine. . . ." [84]—and certain verses of Gallus, particularly Cleopatra's epitaph:

> Thou hast been floating on the o'erswollen stream
>   Of life these many summers; is thy last
> Now over? hast thou dreamt out every dream?
>   Hath horn funereal blown the pageant past?
> Caesar! thou too must follow: all the rods
>   Of sternest lictor cannot scare off Death;
> She claims the earth for heritage; our Gods
>   Themselves have seen their children yield their breath.[85]

This again is the voice of a member of the chorus, the voice of the survivor, the inheritor of history. There is no question that Landor had the dignity required for the handling of a so-called great subject in a so-called great form; he did not have the temperament—perhaps he would have said "the gift": "Far from the footstool of the tragic throne,/I am tragedian in this scene alone."

He was referring to a single, unattached scene entitled "The Shades of Agamemnon and of Iphigeneia," [86] which, in *Pericles and Aspasia,* he has his character Aspasia write. I do not know where he ever came closer to the great tradition of tragedy than in that scene, in which Agamemnon struggles to hide from his daughter the fact that her sweet mother had murdered him. "O Earth!" he exclaims, "I suffered less upon thy shores!" [87] Elysium itself unties the knot and closes over all, and the choruses are grand. Yet what is at the root of its success, even as a tragic scene, is its author's knowledge of domestic fondness. So it has been in the works of Landor discussed in this chapter: we have not met forces but persons, and persons of human rather than heroic stature; the images of grandeur itself have been lyrical; and the observations of ordinary life have lent the warmth of the familiar, speciously, to high and mighty and unlikely doings.

CHAPTER 3

Verse: The Life-Size

I Great Names Domesticated.
Dramatic Lyric

NARRATIVE poetry never ceased to appeal to Landor. He obviously felt at home in what he called "Heroic Idyls," meaning by "Heroic," subject matter of some consequence set forth in heroic verse, and by "Idyl," "a smaller picture of some great picture." He insisted that his use of the latter term was derived from the Idyls of Theocritus himself: "The greater part of Theocritus, and by far the better, does not consist in the loves of shepherds and in their alternating ditties." [1] In Landor's heroic idyls, the greatness or consequence of the picture may be only that of ancient subject matter, or it may be no more than the dignity of patina and of whatever from of old has been touched by venerated hands. There is about his choice of subjects more than a little of the variety that Landor thought one of the tests of greatness: "Sappho, Alcaeus, Anacreon, Phaon," "Theseus and Hippolyta," "The Ancient Idyl: Europa and Her Mother" (the rape of Europa occurs during their dialogue, and never was a wild myth more pleasantly domesticated), "The Trial of Aeschylos," and "Hippomenes and Atalanta."

A hint of how little or much the word "Heroic" truly weighed in Landor's mind may be caught from his use of the title *Idyllia Heroica* for the Latin poems he published in 1820, and from the fact that the collection in English published in 1863 as *Heroic Idyls, with additional poems* was first supposed to be called *Sweepings,* and then *Hellenic Idyls.* Whether his heroic idyls are stories, or conversations, or sketches with commentary, they have it in common to be meditative poems, and the Classical spell is over them.

These poems are built on fact; that is, they are never out of touch with the physical world, whether it is called up to make a character palpable, or celebrated in a free and glad allusion. Outside pure lyric or descriptive verse, the sense of life is seldom so liberally bestowed on poem and reader as in the following lines from "Penelope and Pheido":

> *Pheido.* All the blue figs lie slit upon the wall
> For winter use, and little lizards keep,
> With never-closing eye and panting heart,
> Watch and ward over them against the flies
> And ants, and hold those fast with viscous tongue,
> Sharp-pointed, swiftly out and swiftly in.
> The green and yellow are ungathered yet
> Mostly. Telemakos is tall enough
> To help me up with hand below my heel,
> And shoulder close against the trunk applied.
> *Penelope.* Telemakos plies other work; he mends
> The nets to catch those busy birds that hang
> Tail downward and inflict sad wounds on fig.[2]

Perhaps we are too busy *seeing* to notice that "applied" fails to press our backs against the tree, or to object to the false emphasis brought in by the repetition of sound in "plies" that follows. The passage as a whole warms heart and body with its evidence of things seen. And the first lines vibrate with the music that mere details can make if they are in the right places.

As early as *Gebir,* we knew that Landor looked closely at things. In that poem, even nymphs, whom we are not accustomed to think of as treading on the ground, must cope with an infinitesimal nuisance: ". . . these tuned afresh the shells, / Wiping the green that hoarsen'd them within." [3] This knowledge is uncommon. Other kinds are assumed to be common:

> And now when winter blew the chaff about,
> And hens pursued the grain into the house,
> Quarrelsome and indignant at repulse,
> And rushing back again with ruffled neck,
> They and their brood; and kids blinkt at the brand,
> And bee-nosed oxen, with damp nostrils lowered
> Against the threshold, stampt the dogs away. . . .[4]

The knowledge itself is surely first hand; the convention within which it is communicated is an old one, for Chaucer shows at times the microscopic eye that found for Landor those "bee-nosed oxen": "Chaucer I always loved, for he / Led me to woo fair Poesie." [5] And, in the same connection, we may point to Cowper, of whom Landor says, "Young was I, when from latin lore and greek/I played the truant for thy sweeter Task. . . ./I would become as like thee as I could." [6] Landor had to grow older for real converse with Shakespeare and Milton, but what is worth remarking here is the profound verbal response to Chaucer and to Cowper of a boy who already cherished the wordless creatures of the earth. The author of heroic idyls may, as in "Acon and Rhodope," leave his story line obscure, but he fixes the setting securely on this planet:

> The snow had left the mountain-top; fresh flowers
> Had withered in the meadow; fig and prune
> Hung wrinkling; the last apple glow'd amid
> Its freckled leaves; and weary oxen blinkt
> Between the trodden corn and twisted vine,
> Under whose bunches stood the empty crate,
> To creak ere long beneath them carried home.[7]

And the poem is fragrant with the names of flowers.

A man who notices things seems original, and sometimes the detail in Landor is not only striking in this way, but almost painfully intimate:

> Heard I have
> Boreas and his rude song, and seen the goats
> Stamp on the rock and lick the affrighted eyes
> Of their young kids.[8]

Landor can come equally close to human beings, but he does not linger to collect sensations in the Romantic way. He does not gloat; his poems are neither soft nor cruel; [9] they are not self-indulgent. What he wanted them to be, we may to some extent infer from the differences between the English versions of certain heroic idyls that he first wrote in Latin. I say "differences" rather than "revisions," for he seems to have preferred to rewrite boldly, as if poetry ranked first in importance and translation second. He deals sternly with his own work; passages that a reader may have learned by heart are approached in a new way, or shortened, or erased completely. With Classical rigor, he tears out what calls attention to itself; and this tendency is the most noticeable of his courses of critical action on his own work. Forster too had winced at the surgery. "I remember," he says, "a close he had put to the exquisite *Paris and Oenone* which I thought extremely striking. But no, he said; it ended the poem too much in a flash, which we below were fond of, but which those on the heights of antiquity, both in poetry and prose, avoided." [10] The Landor who can talk and behave in this way is no idolator of Greece and Rome; he is an honest workman who has learned from them something about the nature of the human mind and of human needs.

The line of romance from Virgil to Sir Walter Scott and after may be traced with the bluntest of fingers. There is no difficulty as to what "Catillus and Salia" is about, or roughly what tradition it belongs to. The story does not encourage development of character; like innumerable others throughout history, it requires a Lochinvarical hero, a heroine, an angry father, and a chase. At the end, by a wise turn of our attention, Landor allows us to be sorry for the royal father, who in despair leaps into the river now called the Anio after him. It may be said also that, well before the end, the fugitives (Catillus the hero, Salia the heroine) and we have had a pleasant interlude on the water.

The revised version of this poem is reduced in length by one quarter; but, on the whole, it is a better-written poem, for words are now making more sense and doing more work.[11] When with fright Salia's knees behaved as if they had turned to marble, the poet might have asked himself (he did later): Why marble? why knees? He changed it to "her limbs stiffen to stone." When she does run, the poet has, in revision, first made her *wrench* her feet from where they stood.

"The *Heroic Idylls,* the Hellenics are written in a noble style," said Walter Raleigh, "but they are Culture poems, they breathe of the study." [12] Who could deny it? Yet there are degrees of bookishness; all arts are legacies; and all human craftsmanship must walk a hair line between nature and artifice. In Landor's revision of the following lines from "Catillus and Salia," we can see how the second thoughts of a cultivated and bookish man may not only free his work of such awkwardness as unnecessary repetition ("laboring," "laborious"), but may also cover with cosmetics the wrinkles of life, and subdue unkindly its vulgar noises.

> Soon helmets blaze above the copse; men arm'd
> And unarm'd welcome him; stout hinds belay
> The laboring bark, tugging it where the wind

> Baffles the sail; then, smoking from afield,
> Laborious oxen and stout-hearted steeds.
> But, tho' they aided, slower seem'd the hour
> Than yesterday, when lay the oar athwart
> And the loose sail flapt idly round the mast.

The foregoing was the old version; here is the new:

> He raises up his helm; it lights the copse
> With splendour; soon the rural youth come down
> With oxen reeking from laborious plough,
> And war-horse after his long rest from toil.
> Yet, slower with all these auxiliaries
> The hours moved on than when the oar at eve
> Was thrown upon the thwart, and when the winds
> Had their own will.[13]

Economy, condensation, neatness, sobriety: these are the principles Landor followed; and finally, though the scene is bled pale and nothing is happening in it, the verse has for the ear an effect of sureness, and even a low-keyed charm. I prefer, however, that chest-swelling verse, "Laborious oxen and stout-hearted steeds," which is cliché from end to end, and yet is muscular, loud, and bustling, a part of the action. What restlessness of life we find in the shifting accents from phrase to phrase; what gristle in the language —"smoking" (not "reeking"), "tugging," "belay," "hinds," "baffles," and "stout." And then we have the contrast at the end with one sound persuading us of silence and with one movement defining the motionless.

The finest writing in the world, if relentlessly examined, reveals a mere man's topography of blemishes. So does the renowned perfect surface of Landor's verse; but a good look at the earlier and later versions of these Idyls tells us something we might not have suspected—that, though he often composed in his head (a process that sounds like, though it may not be, a careful one), he was a rapid writer whose imagination, like his temper and his passions, was quick and volatile. What most of the people who have heard of him must think of as the classical, or mortuary, Landorean style is in the longer poems at least, with their diversity of human interest, largely a product of afterthought, of correction, and of revision. There is often, as in the last selection quoted from "Catillus and Salia," a sacrifice not only in spontaneity but in easy, fruitful evocation of particulars.

Another example may be found in two versions of "Coresos and Callirhöe." In the course of suggesting the aftermath of the feast of Bacchus, Landor says:

> Nor after, when short laugh is faintly heard
> Among the bushes, and the star of eve,
> Eve's star and Love's, alone is overhead,
> And shrubs are shaken which no breezes shake,
> Gave he his eyes to sleep, his limbs to rest.

Twelve years later, in 1859, appeared the revision, in which these lines have been altered to

> Not even when Hesper call'd his winking train
> Around him, and when shook the lower shrubs
> More than the breeze had shaken them erewhile,
> Would he decline his aking eyes to sleep. . . .[14]

In trying in the revision to get back to the cool conciseness of his Latin, the poet has failed to do justice to those bushes; the erotic element was overdone, he must have thought to himself—and now there is too little for a reader new to the passage to understand it at all. This kind of absent-minded involvement with the whole line of thought is a common trouble of writers, and a later reading would have discovered it to him.

But we may also compare the two versions of the ending of the poem:

> Cries, clamours, groans, rise, spread. They see the limbs
> Of young Coresos on the earth; and fear
> Seizes them lest they tread that holy blood.
> The temple moans aloud; the city swarms
> With rumours, and the groves and fields around.
> Now 'tis reported that the youth has fallen
> By his own hand to save the virgin; now
> That both were stricken by the fire of heaven.
> With its own violence the crowd is swayed
> Hither and thither, thickening; as the waves
> Conglomerate under the propelling storm.

This time polishing has not meant condensation, but it has, as usual, resulted in concentration:

> Cries and groans are heard,
> And seen upon the pavement where he stood,
> His writhing limbs.
>   With sudden terror flies

The croud bewildered, dreading lest a blood
So sacred should run on and reach their feet.
The temple and the grove around it moan,
And other murmurs, other cries, than rose
So lately, fill the city and the plain.
First flies the rumor that the priest had fallen
By his own hand; it gathered force, and soon
That both were smitten by the wrathful Gods.
From its own weight is that vast multitude
Pusht onward, driven back, conglomerated,
Broken, disperst, like waves on stormy seas.[15]

The blank verse of the first version seems to write itself, and a careless reader might mistake its ease for artlessness until he had
troubled to speak it to himself and gradually to sense the poet's
mastery of rythm. This artistry includes his perfect placing of words
for the desired stress (I instance only "fear" hanging in the air at
the end of the second line and the pounce of "Seizes" at the beginning of the next) and for a physical communication of the action (I
instance "Cŏnglŏm/ ērāte /:/ ūndĕr/ tĥe prŏpēl/ liňg stŏrm/"
when it is set against the normal movements of the iambic
pentameter).

We should be content with the first version, most of all, perhaps,
because of enjoying a certain closeness to the narrator; yet, if the
choice of language in the revision, its tempo, and its rhythm, make
for the distant effect of public utterance, we may for many reasons
admire it more than the other. For instance, we may begin to
wonder if the attractions of the first version are not superficial—
mostly sensuous, a matter of rhythm—or sentimental—when compared with the stoic virtues of the second, in which clarity of images
and their planned conjunction are of first importance; and they,
along with the music, enter upon more of our avenues of consciousness, and thus please us in more ways and with a sense of something firm, four-square, and worthy.

"The Altar of Modesty" loses little in the refining process; it
gains what it can. Poetry itself is seldom, as it is in Keats's "perilous
seas," an effect of revision; clarity and strength often are. And both
may come through expansion rather than condensation, for it is not
conciseness that we desire but clarity, coherence, and strength, of
which conciseness is one of the forms. "The Altar of Modesty" grew
in revision from 298 lines to 315; as revised, it is the result of both

condensation and expansion. Mere obscurities are successfully dealt with, and beyond that, Landor seems to be in pursuit of clarity as a virtue even in portraying the ambiguous.

The subject of the poem is Leda's half maternal, half merely female wish to know what Theseus had done to Helen before her brothers caught up with them and brought her home. The cause of clarity is fairly served in the revision of the following passage in Helen's tale. The first version reads:

> A grove there is, not very far away,
> But hidden from us by the town and hill,
> A gulley runs aside it, which the rains
> May fill in winter, but in summer-time
> Its course is dark with moss and crumbling mould.
> The winds had thrown a rough old tree across
> Whose bark and branches form'd an easy road.
> He saw it, Theseus did, and lept (and made
> Me leap too) from the car: he seated me
> Upon the grass: afraid that I might fear,
> He tried my bosom with such patient hand
> And took such gentle care of me, lest damp
> (The herbs were very damp there) or a stone
> Or broken stick should hurt me. . . .

The second:

>   A grove there is not far
> Beyond the city, but from thence unseen,
> Because the city and the little hill
> Conceal it; there in winter runs a brook,
> But at this season its steep crumbling banks
> Are join'd together by a fallen oak
> The winds have thrown there: boughs and bark afford
> An easy passage over.
>   Theseus lept
> From the low car that bore us: when we reacht
> The farther side, percieving my alarm
> He laid me on the grass, with gentlest hand
> Pressing my bosom to allay my fear,
> And often was it careful to provide
> That neither stick, nor stone beneath, nor bent
> Should harm me; for the bent in woods is stiff.[16]

The impromptu effect of the first version is gone, and with it the youthful parentheses and that engaging "He saw it, Theseus did."

The character of Helen has in the newer version shrunk to what she says; it no longer displays itself to the gallery in miming and tricks of elocution. Landor seems to be saying, "Let us mind the essentials; they are all that Time, our judge, will tolerate. It is better that the words should make enduring verse than that they should abandon themselves in the service of character." And so we readers lose—and a loss it will seem for so long as the spirit of our age may hunger for them—those personal touches which are the evidence of someone speaking who is as helpless and as lovably fumbling as ourselves.

The gentle care of Theseus is now, up to a point, more specifically described; and the whole matter of the dampness is abandoned. That is just as well, for exactly what measures Theseus took to preserve Helen from it was possibly irrelevant, and yet the reader was driven to puzzle over it. But the person preserved, Helen herself, remains, as she ought to do, a little beyond our reach. The bold girl who, when naughty boys called after her, would, with a simplicity impelled by obscure appetite, stop and ask them what they meant—this girl, grown a little under the eyes of Aphrodite, flowers in a dazzle of candor and springtime guile.

Landor in his revision gives us just light enough to be content in the dark. In both versions we see, in Helen's words, Helen's old nurse examine her ("My poor old prying nurse," she adds in the revision, "who really knows/Many things, but imagines she knows more").[17] Jubilant, the nurse proclaims her preserved from harm or shame. Helen makes no comment on this conclusion or on the nurse's mockery of the prowess of Theseus; she simply reports the incident in lively terms, and in the revision, when she ends her narrative, Landor calls her "the unwary maid." In another addition in his own words, after Helen's account of Theseus' gentleness with her, Landor describes her as going on with her story "somewhat less dissembling." [18] None of this ambiguity sounds in the poem like mere factitious mystification; it brings to life some of the paradoxes of self-knowledge. Helen is a girl; and one of Landor's best afterthoughts is eight new lines in which he specifically shows her in a normal young daughter's moment of need for the warm intimacy—for the breast, the arms, of the mother.[19] By it, the whole poem is strengthened.

The lament of Theseus at his loss of Helen may be in the revision slightly less ambiguous than before—love torn from one's open arms upon the threshold does seem to mean love unconsummated;

but the pair had been absent a considerable while; and in any case the threshold was where Theseus felt it to be. If pressed for the whole story, our author might admit that Helen must remain acceptable to Menelaus and also that the gods are great. It is not his duty to tell us more, and his revisions make this clear. The poem is his own; it does not belong to any of the gossips quoted by Pierre Bayle. Rising from the book, we take with us a Helen born for her fable. As for mystery and knowledge, who is to read a blush on the cheek of Aphrodite?

In revising the passage that describes the nurse's examination of Helen, Landor seems to have intended to adapt it for the England of 1859. It no longer offers the painter a Helen disrobed, with one knee thrown over her couch: not only is there no painting, there is not even a pose. As a consequence, the verse takes longer to communicate the idea, and rather than being entertained, the reader is detained beyond what he may consider to be reason. Thus, in the early version, the candor of nudity had been the guard of decency.[20] A similar change is in some apparently ingenuous words of Helen recommending that Theseus content himself with friendship. Her comparison of the ardor and compliancy of his friend Pirithöus with the same qualities in Ganymede and Hyacinthus is removed; her evocations of their beauty remain.

In both these instances there is a loss of the specific; and not, I think, so much out of deference to the aura of Queen Victoria as simply because in Landor's times that kind of specification tended to call attention to itself. In other words, in standing out, it marred the harmony of his page. In another speech of Helen's an image of the first version is similarly suppressed in the revised one:

> Never, when any hurt me, did I bite
> Or scratch; I only trembled as, when all
> The strings of harp or lyre are swept at once,
> Water runs trembling to the vase's rim.

In this passage, one simile climbs upon the back of another; we might be expected to settle for trembling in the strings or for vibration in the instrument, and to object to the water image as a favorite brain child wastefully reared. But the latter comes much closer to expressing experience of emotion, as distinguished from physical reaction. The revised lines read:

> your Helena was taught
> Far different manners, nor would, even tho hurt,

Use tooth or nail, but tremble as the strings
Of a lyre tremble if swept all at once.[21]

I regret losing the water image, though I admit that it was too
interesting merely in itself, that it was arrived at in a willful and
roundabout way, and that it evoked not only a sensitive Helen but
a tearful one—and that was very wrong of it. But, in the revision,
we are given nothing to repair its loss.

This kind of critical response, which tends to clutch to the
bosom every moment of pleasure, whether drugged or lunatic, has
for more than a century and a half been not unknown. It is not, as
some may think, an impulse of Romantic despair; it is only the
normal healthy pagan instinct, in an uncertain world, to get what
can be got from the passing moment. This sort of response, then,
is more respectable than it seems. That which we may agree to call
instinct is not sentimental; nor is it in itself irrational. It is a kind
of immediate judgment, without which life would stop almost before it began. What we think of as the rational mind manifests itself
in the next stage: a place of pause or second thoughts, where a man
may begin to respect himself—and where the arts begin to flourish.
Second thoughts told Landor what must be sacrificed if these poems
were to stand scrutiny—if, in other words, they were to stand. What
we are invited to sacrifice in poetry, as in life, is a specious pleasure
for a lasting satisfaction, a specious freedom for the freedom of
second thoughts.

In all his work there is no harder test of the purposes of the poet
Landor than is set by the two English versions of "Corythos." The
subtitle of the Latin version (Idyl V) had been "The Death of
Paris and Oenone," but in the 1847 English poem Landor's emphasis of sympathy and interest goes to their son Corythos, whom
Oenone sends to melt his father's heart and bring him back to her.
The young man is so like his father that Helen knows him. Sympa-
thetically, she prepares a meeting of father and son; but, at first
sight of the hesitant stranger, dressed in a garment once woven for
Menelaos, Paris slashes him to death. The poem goes on to relate
the father's discovery that he has murdered his son, his being shot
with the fated arrows of Philoctetes, his return to Oenone, and the
death of them together. If telling this whole story was what Landor
had in mind, it had to be revised so that it did not seem to end
with the funeral of Corythos. In the 1859 version, therefore, we
are kept at a little distance from Corythos; he is a likable young

man, but the charming proofs of his youthfulness and sweetness of character are resolutely suppressed so that we may be sufficiently struck with the horror and the pathos and yet expect to accompany Paris to his final moment and Oenone's. The 1847 version is warm, breathless, moving—all in the accents of one who has just come from the scene. Landor appears to have been willing to reject it altogether, rather than try to save the best passages and piece them into a new version. The moods of the two are different: the 1859 version is cool and polished, with nothing of the heart-catching intimacy of the one of 1847.

With emphasis on the larger story comes a more contemplative view of Helen, when, for instance, the lines "One who could place herself amid the low, / Could smile with them and weep with them, and view / On the same level all, herself above / All things the world's eternal walls contain" are raised and refined to "All in her sight were level, for she stood / High above all within the seagirt world." [22] The picture of Corythos entering his father's presence is far better in the 1847 version, but it placed Corythos himself in the center of the scene and of our feelings. The action as revised is swifter, more tacit; and the scene ends with a real "curtain." In the first version more than a hundred lines later, we had been gathered to the side of wounded Paris by means of the fine and sudden detail we have before noted:

> And as they bear him thither, toiling up
> The narrow path, often the loose round stones
> Slip under them and shake him, often spring
> The branches back and strike against his wound.

This passage is improved by dramatic focusing and restraint:

> . . . Down the narrow and steep path are heard
> The pebbles rattling under peasants' feet,
> Whose faces the dense shrubs at every side
> Smite as they carry on his bier the man
> Who thinks his journey long. . . .[23]

But what is to recompense us for the line in which the grief-struck father, at the cooling funeral pyre, separates "The ashes of the boughs and of the boy"? The revision reads: "So from the brittle brands he swept away/The whiter ashes." [24] This substitute has its own beauty, both remote and touching; but it cannot take the place of that consummate line which, even as he wrote it,

Landor had left hanging in the middle of a sentence, as if to strip
it of its power to draw us to it, and all words to a close.

The range of these poems includes the pathos of "Corythos" and
the Prior-like froth of "Damaetas and Ida," the latter in teasing
tetrameter couplet. It also includes the heights of poetry, and somewhere on those heights is Homer's dream, in the second section of
Landor's "Homer, Laertes, Agatha":

> *Laertes.* Hast thou slept well, Maeonides?
>> *Homer.* I slept
> Three hours ere sunrise, 'tis my wont, at night
> I lie awake for nearly twice as long.
> *Laertes.* Ay; singing birds wake early, shake their plumes,
> And carol ere they feed. Sound was thy sleep?
> *Homer.* I felt again, but felt it undisturb'd,
> The pelting of the little curly waves,
> The slow and heavy stretch of rising billows,
> And the rapidity of their descent.
> I thought I heard a Triton's shell, a song
> Of sylvian Nymph, and laughter from behind
> Trees not too close for voices to come thro',
> Or beauty, if Nymph will'd it, to be seen;
> And then a graver and a grander sound
> Came from the sky, and last a long applause.[25]

When Landor's mind is in Greece, all the song there is in the man
is stirred. Away from the wranglings of a Christian Europe, back in
imagination in a time before his most furious preoccupations had
been prepared for him, what an effortless heathen he makes, and
how he dilates at ease! It is odd that the two Englishmen who have
best known Pan—Landor and Thomas Love Peacock—both celebrated him, at a mature age, in the middle of the nineteenth century. (Norman Douglas was not an Englishman, but he was born so
little later that he might almost have been blessed by them.)

In "Pan and Pitys" and "Cupid and Pan," from which in revision
Landor smoothes away roughnesses that could have been felt only
by the fine hand of a craftsman, readers may share specifically in
Landor's knowledge of the god. As usual, the later versions tend to
be more reticent, and to pause or particularize only for the sake
of the larger idea; in these poems the lyricism grows more intense
by correction and is sometimes wider in its reach. Out of second
thought came the deep tones of Pan, "the grave Arcad," warding off

the unruly Cupid and any contest between them: ". . . check yet awhile/Ferocious beauty." [26]

In the sunnier spots of Arcady, the senses of Landor are equally alert. Richard Aldington once commented on some phrases of Landor's that come from the passage in "Lysander, Alcanor, Phanöe" beginning "In spring we garland him with pointed flowers":

> "Pointed flowers," "sweet-breathing mountain strawberry," "stiff nar-
> row olive-leaves"—are not such phrases the very marrow of Theo-
> critus? Is it only a romantic fancy which makes one feel that no
> poets were ever so sensitive to the crisp outlines and clear tints of
> flowers and fruits as the Greeks? Landor shared that exquisite plastic
> feeling. Only a poet who is so gifted with the love and understanding
> of their beauty can so evoke their essential form and colour and scent.
> The demi-gods whom the Greek poets invented as the spirits of flowers
> and trees and windy rocks were a projection of this sensitiveness. And
> Landor, the tender old Englishman, understood so well that delicate
> respect for beauty.[27]

That respect is found in his portraits of young girls, and the girls respond by stepping out of their frames. How excellent these portrayals are, too few people seem to know. At eighty-nine, Landor drew another Helen, this last time for "The Marriage of Helena and Menelaos." His suggestions of the state of mind of Helena, aged sixteen, child and woman, loath and less than loath, are exquisitely delicate and well found. She stays in the mind, "paddling listlessly" in the river, where "some irksomeness/ She felt which water could not all remove"; and seated in hall with her elders:

> Often did she look forward, to drive off
> The flies that buzz'd about the stranger's head . . .
> Flies never were so troublesome before.[28]

The whole poem tells of an aged poet who has not grown old, who has not even changed, since middle age, in imagination or style. The poem also gives proof of his native Classical sureness when his mind is on the main subject and he is not too consciously a rival of the Latin poets.

> She ran across the court wherein three steeds
> Were standing loose; there Polydeukes trimm'd
> His courser's mane, there Kastor drew his palm
> Down the pink nostril of his dapple-gray,

And just beyond them the Thessalian steed
Stampt at neglect, for Menelaos lay
Sleepless past sunrise, which was not his wont.[29]

There is not a superfluous ounce of information; each detail is just
and satisfying. Each figure is still moving—and yet all are caught
in eternal attitudes, and all spaced with the morning air flowing full
among them.

This poetic eye, so busy about hearth and courtyard, is the same
that is so learned in groves and gardens. Among things seen, the
mind—which is the eye turned critic—decides what, for composition, for harmony of things, is to be married to what other. Above
all, the mind decides what to leave out—not as a rejection of un-
pleasing fact, for that which is now rejected will be called by the
poet to shine tomorrow—but what to leave out for the sake of seeing clearly. I have used the word "Classical" to describe Landor's
management of these things at his best, and the term may stretch
from Hellenic to Hellenistic; but it is more to the point to allow the
poet himself to take us back to Theocritus:

                              Pan
          Pan led me to a wood the other day,
          Then, bending both hoofs under him, where moss
          Was softest and where highest was the tuft,
          Said he, "sit thou aside me; there is room
          Just for us two; the tinklers are below
          To catch the little birds and butterflies,
          Nor see us nor would heed us if they saw.
          I minded thee in Sicily with one
          I dearly love; I heard thee tell my loss
          Of Pitys; and he swore that none but thou
          Could thus contend with him, or ever should.
          Though others had loud lyres and struck them well,
          Few could bring any harmony from reeds
          By me held high, and higher since thou hast breath'd
          Thy gentle breath o'er Pitys and her Pan."

Harmony from reeds: it is a proud and humble boast.

II   *Variety: The Critical Muse*

Few English poets can have made more spontaneous music
than Landor did, or have been more at home in a demanding
craft. Landor could do almost anything in verse that the English

language can do, and half a dozen experiments in hexameters go almost beyond that limit. That even at the end he could hardly keep himself from versifying is attested to by Kate Field, who preserved for us a few of his impromptu rhymes that came out in conversation with her in his last days:

"Advising me with regard to certain rules in my Latin Grammar he exclaimed—

> "What you'd fain know, you will find;
> What you want not leave behind." [30]

What he wanted to say found its frame: heroic couplet ("Guidone and Lucia," for instance—unexceptionable, if little more); Alcaic ode ("To Lamartine"); anapaestic tetrameter couplet ("An Address to the Fellows of Trinity College"); a three-line stanza grown out of dactylic dimeter:

> O Father Matthew!
> Whatever path you
> In life pursue,
>
> God grant your Reverence
> May brush off never hence
> Our mountain dew! [31]

Though Landor was particularly fond of saying a thing in less than a page of blank verse, he indulged in what seem to be—but, if they were worth counting, would turn out not to be—an endless number of shapes of stanza, rhyming more often than not in couplets but diverse in their pattern of length of line. Free verse he tried as early as 1800 in his pretended translations from Arabic and Persian. Unlike other nineteenth-century poets, however, he avoided the sonnet throughout his life. He may have written one—a translation from Alfieri [32]—but his feelings about the form are as striking as its absence from the body of his work: "A sonnet? Never." Sonnets are to be written in Italian, which overflows with rhyme and consequently with such "warm-water" verse: [33]

> No, I will never weave a sonnet,
> Let others wear their patience on it;
> A better use of time I know
> Than tossing shuttles to and fro. [34]

He delighted in old meters (as he said at the end of some English hexameters), but they belong in the country and climate where they were born; for, ". . . than pamper them here I would rather/Tie up my Pegasus tight to the scanty-fed rack of a sonnet." [35]

Landor seems not to balk so much at the infernal difficulty of rhyme in English as he does at the mere idea of any constraints but those independently self-imposed. It is true that his nature forbids him to parade in conventional costume or to show that he too can write in rime royal or the Spenserian stanza. Where form or shape in his verse is such that it must be noticed, as in his quatrains, nevertheless shape, image, and music may imperceptibly slip away under the grasp of the senses, blend, and be lost in a translucent thought. Landor follows his nature; he is a poet, a thinker, not a filler-in of forms. His subject matter is that of a man who responds with animation to what he meets in the course of a day—political men and events, his reading, his friends, and the small ephemera that go unobserved except by the poetic mind.

A response is either critical or vacuous; even *Hallelujah!* presumably has its reasons. Much of what Landor has to say is unfavorable criticism; but, insofar as satire is one of those *forms* of literature, and its requirements and its delights as a form tend to take precedence over the thing said, his habit is to eschew it. At the age of twenty, he avers that he hates the form of a satire.[36] At fifty-six, he succumbs momentarily in "Epistle to a Barrister"; it is a heavy piece with a fair amount of ambiguous distant thunder in it. At sixty-one, he produces a 355-line exercise called "A Satire on Satirists, and admonition to detractors"; it yields a neat epigram— "If there were living upon earth but twain,/One would be Abel and the other Cain"; and a sigh—"Satire! I never called thee very fair." [37]

Landor's own way is simply to attack, to say what he thinks, and to say it as well as he can. His attack is perforce imaginative, as in "Espousals of H. M. of Portugal": [38]

> Youngster of Coburg! thou hast found a throne
> Easy to mount, and easier to slip down:
> But, in the name of wonder! who beside
> Of mortal men could mount thy royal bride?
> So vast an enterprize requires the force
> And ladder too that scaled the Trojan horse,
> In whose rank orifice some hundreds hid

> Themselves and arms, and down the rampire slid.
> Thou hast achieved a mightier deed and bolder,
> And hast not dislocated hip or shoulder.

The touch of rowdiness, somewhat rare, is always welcome if only as a reminder that the eighteenth century was still alive in its living children. Ageless, perhaps, though placed by Wheeler in a section of the poems entitled by him "Senilia," is this small matter from the quarrel with Mrs. Yescombe:

> Cadmus! if you should want again
> Some dragons teeth to sow the plain,
> Haste hither: one old woman has
> A bushel in a pan of brass.
> Mind! do not throw the foam away,
> Keep it to kill the birds of prey.
> Its virulence exceeds the might
> Of hellebore and aconite.[39]

This poem is intemperate, not senile. And the next-to-last couplet must have made the angry old man erupt into laughter.

The story that Landor, upon throwing his cook out the window, exclaimed, "Good God, I forgot the tulips!" [40] is proof enough that he was both an artist and a man of humor. Humor is an elusive subject and one as infinitely ranging as poetry itself; nevertheless, a few illustrations of overt humor in Landor's verse might be welcome. In all his work the examples are comparatively few; but they range from the homespun of

> A Sensible Girl's Reply to Moore's
> *"Our couch shall be roses all spangled with dew"*

> It would give me rheumatics, and so it would you—[41]

to so polished a product of thought and craft as the following:

> The burden of an ancient rhyme,
> Is, "By the forelock seize on Time."
> Time in some corner heard it said;
> Pricking his ears, away he fled;
> And, seeing me upon the road,
> A hearty curse on me bestow'd.
> "What if I do the same by thee?
> How wouldst thou like it?" thunder'd he,
> And, without answer thereupon,
> Seizing *my* forelock . . it was gone.[42]

It takes a properly serious man to understand the value of a trifle;
Landor is surely such a man, but in the verbal sense he is no ironist
—and he knows it:

> Irony is the imp of wit,
> The truly witty banish it.
> Where are the mountebank and clown
> Who cannot turn things upside down? [43]

He knows it without quite understanding irony, which is partly a
game at the expense of the slow-witted—as H. W. Fowler's wit
reveals [44]—but is more than anything else a poetic delight in absurdity, one sprung from depths where anger and pity meet. That
is why, as a manifestation of critical mind, irony is immortal. It is
instantly creative and self-delighting as any god and delicate as the
human spirit. Like Proteus or any poor player, it assumes all shapes
that please it; but they are shapes of this world, loved ephemeral
ones—and, when it is harsh or bitter, it is so for their sake.

Landor at eighty-three said that he had read Swift's *Tale of a
Tub* more often than any other prose work in the language: "What
a writer!" [45] He was speaking of Swift as he might have spoken of
Shakespeare; he was reading him better than some twentieth-
century professor on the prowl for paradox and for the numberless
antitheses in nature that he calls "irony," but that, instead, are
simple evidences of the range of life, and of its heartbeat. Irony is
a matter of temperament and early influences; like a tone of voice,
like a shift in the breeze, it is nothing to write a treatise about. And,
if Landor was so unlucky as to have been born into a heavy-footed
household, his reader seldom suffers on that account.

Not being an ironist does not prevent a poet from making poetry
out of amusing or provocative contrasts. One of Landor's pleasant-
est is that of "The Gardener and the Mole." The Mole, caught by
the Gardener, is said by Landor to reply *meekly* in self-defense, but
a meekness that could cut down the pretensions of mankind demands a control of ironic speech that is beyond Landor; without
any sense of loss, he gives his Mole the poet's own freedom of
frontal attack. The Mole is talkative to a fault, and his "home-
brought truths" cause the Gardener, though by nature a mild man,
to stop him by cutting off his head. The Mole's condemnation of
mankind is not particularly vigorous, but we are rather grateful to
the little fellow and ready to concede that, harm for harm, that

which is done by him is both small and natural. The whole of the little fable is told with the gravity that its brand of humor requires, and the stroke of violence descends with brevity and composure.

The following untitled poem is humor in full dress:

> Yes; I write verses now and then,
> But blunt and flaccid is my pen,
> No longer talked of by young men
>   As rather clever:
>
> In the last quarter are my eyes,
> You see it by their form and size;
> Is it not time then to be wise?
>   Or now or never.
>
> Fairest that ever sprang from Eve!
> While Time allows the short reprieve,
> Just look at me! would you believe
>   'Twas once a lover?
>
> I can not clear the five-bar gate,
> But trying first its timber's state,
> Climb stiffly up, take breath, and wait
>   To trundle over.
>
> Thro' gallopade I can not swing
> The entangling blooms of Beauty's spring;
> I can not say the tender thing,
>   Be't true or false,
>
> And am beginning to opine
> Those girls are only half-divine
> Whose waists yon wicked boys entwine
>   In giddy waltz.
>
> I fear that arm above that shoulder,
> I wish them wiser, graver, older,
> Sedater, and no harm if colder
>   And panting less.
>
> Ah! people were not half so wild
> In former days, when, starchly mild,
> Upon her high-heel'd Essex smiled
>   The brave Queen Bess.[46]

This light verse is of the deftest—and for the intimacy under the gloved control of steely intellect we must go back to Prior. The beery lament that nothing is as it was, that with youth goes everything, is now reconceived in champagne. The humor of unconscious self-caricature owes a good deal to the listener's uncertainty, to his feeling that intelligence so happily befogged may at any moment break through, take command, and spoil the play. Landor's artistic assurance makes for more than the usual tenseness of this kind; his triple rhymes, with their suggestion of "and then, and then," fit the speaker's impulsive confidences blurted to himself; and the short fourth lines, firmly helpless, rhyme all the stanzas together. Of use on the side of champagne and strength are the charm and vigor of "trundle," and of "starchly mild," and the fact that they do not stare at us from the page. And the contrast with Elizabethan days is delightfully apoplectic in its inspiration, while being in its expression polite, grave, and fond.

With a few exceptions of poems that may be labeled as humor, Landor's sense of humor lives along with, and qualifies, his sense of everything else. As a guide, it lies deep in the mind, imparting, as only it can do, the sense of proportion.

That sense of proportion is nowhere more desperately needed than in politics, which deadens it; and a large number of Landor's poems are political. How much of the time and genius Landor spent upon this subject was wasted, we cannot justly say, for his warm response to it was evidence of his being in his own way alive. Indeed, few readers of our day are so thoroughly versed in nineteenth-century affairs as to discover themselves in Landor's highly topical praise or blame of the fourteenth Earl of Derby, George Canning, the Marchese di Azeglio, Daniele Manin, the eleventh Earl of Dalhousie, Prince Menschikoff, Sir James Graham, Prince Adam Czartoriski, "President Pierce and Bomba King." That the reader knows something of Andrew Jackson, Louis Napoleon, Garibaldi, and Louis Kossuth is a help. What in Landor's political verse meets us more than halfway is the lifelong fierceness of his sense of justice.

Indignation and a sufficient liveliness of language, along with recognition of the perennial nature of his subject, keep "A Foren Ruler" bitterly fresh for our own day:

> He says, *My reign is peace,* so slays
> A thousand in the dead of night.

> *Are you all happy now?* he says,
>   And those he leaves behind cry *quite.*
> He swears he will have no contention,
>   And sets all nations by the ears;
> He shouts aloud, *No intervention!*
>   Invades, and drowns them all in tears.[47]

Landor's hatred of tyrants and his activity in behalf of a Kossuth must be, not qualified, but clarified by such lines as he wrote when the Municipal Council at Tours declared for Louis Napoleon:

> Men will be slaves; let them; but force them not;
> To force them into freedom is stil worse;
> In one they follow their prone nature's bent,
> But in the other stagger all awry,
> Blind, clamorous, and with violence overthrow
> The chairs and tables of the untasted feast.
> Bastiles are reconstructed soon enough,
> Temples are long in rising, once cast down. . . .

Then he speaks of those who promise to rebuild for us, if we agree to be ruled body and soul; who will cleanse us from "inborn sin" and tell us, at a price, how to die so as to cheat the devil.[48] An angrier poem, and a better one—about an aspect of politics called "religion"—is "The Pigeon-Fancier":

> Some are fanciers in religions,
> Some (the wiser they) in pigeons.
> I confess it, I prefer
> Much the pigeon-fancier.
> For I never knew him spill
> Pigeon's blood, nor threaten ill,
> Whether hell's or kitchen's flame . .
> Can those others say the same?
> Fools! to fancy loads of faggot
> Are required to cook a maggot! [49]

The discovery that something can be made of the not very thought-provoking accident that "pigeon" rhymes with "religion," might have ended there—in a poem shakily based on a slight accident. But what happens is that we move logically and, in terms of the imagination, with a surprising inevitability, from a drawling joke to a sword thrust into the heart of the subject. Mere common sense—with a little of just the right heightening of light and shade and just the right suppression of all but essentials—comes to us with the swiftness of wit and with the rounded weight of truth. It would be inconvenient were someone to tack that last couplet on to the façade of Dante's *Inferno*.

Landor more than once has wrung from unpromising subject matter something worth the labor. In "Greece! Be Tolerant," are two of the supreme lines of all his work: "Whatever stands must fall; the dust alone/We trample on rises and keeps its form." In another poem on Greece, published nearly thirty years after Landor's death, is what has to have been an early intimation of the idea—that only dust remains unchanged:

> . . . Earth's proud giant brood, they lie
> Along the dust; the dust alone remains
> Imperishable and by age unchanged.[50]

The idea, coming in the last three words, seems an afterthought, and we can feel him fumbling with it; the motions are tentative but wasteful; the idea is not unwelcome, but it is a dead weight carried along on mere verse or metered prose. If we compare this passage— this idea (for ideas cannot be the same if a word is different)— with the beautiful one first quoted, we see "trample" and then the rising from being trampled, which more than matches the fall; and then we wonder at the mingling of truth and dream, the enduring substance of the "insubstantial pageant," the eternity of cloud shape in its change, the dust that "keeps its form."

In the same region of consummate things is Landor's poem in which he joins a great company of lovers—to Elizabeth, Queen of Hearts: "The Mother of Prince Rupert." A fine poem through-out, it ends with a cadence of incomparable loveliness:

> Sole one of all thy race
> Who never brought disgrace
>   Upon thy native land!
> Against the ruin'd wall
> Where rang thy marriage-hall,
>   Now still as heaven, I stand,
> And think upon thy son,
> Who many laurels won
>   Where laurels should not grow,
> Til England's star prevail'd
> And Caledonia's paled,
>   And the dim crown lay low.[51]

Any poet would have thanked Apollo for his gift of the word "dim" and for the ear that so perfectly resolved, in the last line, that doomful and reluctant fall.

Landor's other main subject of comment in verse is, as Wheeler has it, "Books and Writers." "I own I like plain dishes best," Landor said, when testifying to his pleasure in Goldsmith and Gray.[52] Though he honored Spenser, it was Chaucer whom he loved as a friend: "No bodyless and soulless elves/I seek, but creatures like ourselves." [53] Such a preference includes most of the finest company, from Homer and Aristophanes to Molière and La Fontaine. The fortunes of Wordsworth in the mind and affections of Landor would require a pamphlet to follow, but irritation and amusement at both his character and his work never obscured for him Wordsworth's greatness. He wrote the following about him and Byron in 1845:

> Byron's sharp bark and Wordsworth's long-drawn wheese
> Issue alike from breasts that pant for ease.
> One caught the fever of the flowery marsh,
> The other's voice intemperate scorn made harsh.
> But each hath better parts: to One belong
> Staffs for the old and guide-posts for the young:
> The Other's store-room downcast eyes approve,
> Hung with bright feathers dropt from moulting Love.[54]

Landor doffed his hat to the work of Keats and of Shelley; Southey, of whom he had much to say, had been, when Landor most needed him, his guide through the shades, "trustier far" than Dante's.[55] But Landor's critical opinions are best left for discussion with his prose. Two poems on literary men deserve quotation in full, because in their different ways they rise above special interest and bookish allusion: the first is about Robert Burns; the second, Robert Browning.

> Had we two met, blythe-hearted Burns,
>   Tho water is my daily drink,
>   May God forgive me but I think
> We should have roared out toasts by turns.
>
> Inquisitive low-whispering cares
>   Had found no room in either pate,
>   Until I asked thee, rather late,
> Is there a hand-rail to the stairs? [56]

Those foreign, intrusive, and skulking cares that worm their way into heads not full of glad companionship are, as Landor draws them, admirable; but nothing is more so than the convivial force and tuneful simplicity of the whole. The poem "To Robert Browning," composed of fourteen reined-in lines of strong and musical blank verse, may stand with the best sonnets in English:

> There is delight in singing, though none hear
> Beside the singer; and there is delight
> In praising, though the praiser sit alone
> And see the prais'd far off him, far above.
> Shakespeare is not *our* poet, but the world's,
> Therefore on him no speech; and short for thee,
> Browning! Since Chaucer was alive and hale,
> No man hath walk'd along our roads with step
> So active, so inquiring eye, or tongue
> So varied in discourse. But warmer climes
> Give brighter plumage, stronger wing; the breeze
> Of Alpine heights thou playest with, borne on
> Beyond Sorrento and Amalfi, where
> The Siren waits thee, singing song for song.[57]

A reader might profitably leaf through the *Poems* to see what a genius Landor had for first lines, for beginnings. And his endings are quietly superb. In the modest middles of these bookman's poems' succinct (well-belted) muscular phrases catch the mind: "High-crested Scott, broad-breasted Burns"; [58] "Humour's pink primate, Sydney Smith." [59] It is clear enough that Landor does not require much room to write in.

III *Epigram*

Criticism and comment in verse must bite into the mind, and we have been noticing the incisiveness of Landor's. As we might expect, he took naturally to epigram; and, in much of what he had to say, the intellectual rewards contented him. Not only a Classical training but a Classical ease of mind is in his simple statement about this matter: "Our only aim has been to fit/A ready rhyme to ready wit." [60] The transparent modesty is everybody's; but the calm, the unbedeviled pride of a good workman, is a state to which no other temperament aspires.

Landor's subjects in these little poems are whatever comes to mind: a paperweight, the desire to be let alone, the rind and the fruit, wisdom and the loss of memory, the striking of an egg with another egg, honeymoons, Julian the Apostate, idleness, a sphinx, a prude. Epigrams from his early and his later days, undated, sit comfortably on the page together. Some might be considered by a purist as nothing more than a brace of gnomic lines; others are epigrams in everyone's use of the term. The following poem might be considered prefatory to the rest:

> Poet! I like not mealy fruit; give me
> Freshness and crispness and solidity;
> Apples are none the better over-ripe,
> And prime buck-venison I prefer to tripe.[61]

The literary preference is especially pleasing when it so critically and fittingly describes both the literary form and the individual poem the description is in. The form itself, being a summary one, tends briefly to dispose of one subject and briefly to memorialize another. Thus, on the unkinder side, wit finds a resemblance worth a few moments' play:

> Alas! 'tis very sad to hear.
> Your and your Muse's end draws near:
> I only wish, if this be true,
> To lie a little way from you.
> The grave is cold enough for me
> Without you and your poetry.[62]

If this passage seems a little ragged, the reason is that Landor has been a trifle too leisurely: a joke may be too long about it. More a matter of word than of idea is the following:

> In the odor of sanctity Miriam abounds,
> Her husband's is nearer the odor of hounds,
> With a dash of the cess-pool, a dash of the sty,
> And the water of cabbages running hard-by.[63]

Were it not for the enthusiasm, our occasional human pleasure in well-regulated excess, and, certainly, the choice of "abounds," these lines would be poor stuff.

Wit in anger has found in "A Quarrelsome Bishop" two kinds of clawing creature, one more decent than the other:

> To hide her ordure, claws the cat;
> You claw, but not to cover that.
> Be decenter, and learn at least
> One lesson from the cleanlier beast.[64]

The quatrain is not unsuccessful, but "ordure" may seem more expressive of the author's feelings than descriptive of anything. The lines are sharp and swift, and to finish a man off with a piece of kindly advice is not in the power of us all. The following quatrain, from *Pericles and Aspasia,* is more satisfying; indeed, it is a perfect epigram of Martial's kind:

> Leave me thy head when thou art dead,
>   Speusippus! Prudent farmers say
> An ass's skull makes plentiful
> The poorest soil; and ours is clay.[65]

What epigrams must *not* be, Landor tells us:

> Epigrams must be curt, nor seem
> Tail-pieces to a poet's dream.
> If they should anywhere be found
> Serious, or musical in sound
> Turn into prose the two worst pages
> And you will rank among the sages.[66]

More of his epigrams than not lean toward the lyric, for he was a poet, not just a commentator with a gift for the laconic. And what is a more natural response to the rhythmic variety of life than music?—as Landor himself tells us:

> When I gaze upon the sky
> And the sea below, I cry,
> Thus be poetry and love,
> Deep beneath and bright above.[67]

Seldom does a poem so beautifully demonstrate that reason and passion, intellect and feeling, are aspects of a single consciousness, and that, when we most clearly see, we are not divided.

At least one Landor epigram is destroyed, however, by the splendor of a single line. Landor begins by saying of Death that he indiscriminately gathers "The flowering children and rough-rinded fathers" [68]—and the last couplet cannot be made to matter. The wonder of the line is not only in the imaginative force of its last image, and in the splicing together of the sounds, but in the coherence and justice of all the parts of the idea. Poetry is a result of proper thinking.

IV *Lyric*

When we find epigrams like this one—

> From you, Ianthe, little troubles pass
>   Like little ripples down a sunny river;
> Your pleasures spring like daisies in the grass,
>   Cut down, and up again as blithe as ever.[69]

or this one—

> Tears driven back upon the fountain-head,
>   And Sorrow's voice supprest,
> Heave, while in quiet sleep repose the dead.
>   Oh! when will they too rest! [70]—

we have found epigram in the full stream of lyric poetry. Saintsbury called Landor "hardly second to Ben Jonson" in "his smaller lyrics (epigrammatic in the Greek rather than in the modern sense)." [71] The qualities of "Rose Aylmer," the most famous of these, are, as in all fine making, not easy to isolate:

> Ah what avails the sceptred race,
>   Ah what the form divine!
> What every virtue, every grace!
>   Rose Aylmer, all were thine.
> Rose Aylmer, whom these wakeful eyes
>   May weep, but never see,
> A night of memories and of sighs
>   I consecrate to thee.[72]

What are the parts and ingredients of perfection? Originality of idea, of form, of style—probably never; for perfection dawns upon us as a kind of self-realization. The original, or individual, in any but the sense in which we are all originals, draws us apart by singularity. Like "Drink to me only with thine eyes," "Rose Aylmer" is a final version, a resting place of old ideas and phrases that have found at last their happy relationship, their music, and, in the truth of it, are new for ever.

What can be analyzed? "Rose Aylmer" is a song woven of long vowel sounds. Perhaps it is fatuous to hear in it *Oh!* as well as *Ah!;* and the sharp *ā* not only of *Aylmer* but of *wail;* the germane sounds of the diphthong *Ai!,* the ancient and nearly worldwide cry of pain, and, lastly, of *Ay me!* At least the notes come to us, and differently come again, in exquisite order. And the softer last note of *thee* comes naturally out of the louder long *i* by movement of thought: *eyes* that may *weep* but may not *see;* here is an inevitability, a birth and growth of idea, picture, and sound together, one for which most poets must labor their lives away in vain.

And what of the self-containment, the dignity of the poem, by which it sings in stone? In the first line, *avails* locks itself by sound to *race* and sets firmly before us the first wide view of helpless mortality: her race was *sceptred,* and worldly power—even ancient, historical, and now present in the blood—is powerless in the face of death. Then we turn to the other kind of power, not earthly but godlike, the "form divine," that must lose divinity as well as the strength to live. So with every virtue, every grace—all are hers, those essences of will and fortune by which we raise ourselves from the dust only to fall at last. Then comes her name and a miracle of restraint, of tenderness in elegiac distance. The poet's eyes are *these* eyes, less personal than *mine,* eyes not *sleepless* but *wakeful,* which could not fail to see what they stay awake for, were that object to be seen, but recognize her in the one way that is left: in the submissive blindness of tears. Then finally we have the note of commemoration, the votive gift of thoughts past and present—and the word *consecrate,* humble yet radiant with the poet's refusal to call merely mortal what was divine enough for him.

The lyrics, short and long, are various enough to give a great deal of pleasure to those who like verse. Landor can offer us, in "I will not call her fair," a perfect piece of the seventeenth century, stylistically unmistakable, that is prosodically more brilliant than its exemplars. In manner and costume, he ranges from a full-dress "The crysolites and rubies Bacchus brings," to an informal "Thou needst not pitch upon my hat." There are pleasant trifles— "Pursuits! alas, I now have none"—which, if in idea they amount to little, do, in the charm of craftsmanship, amount to much. Though Landor is not like Herrick, he has something of Herrick's utter ease; and this is remarkable in one who impresses most readers as a carver of language. In the following poem, we find no trace of effort; it flows from its source without halt or change of direction:

> Dull is my verse: not even thou
> Who movest many cares away

> From this lone breast and weary brow,
>   Canst make, as once, its fountain play;
> No, nor those gentle words that now
>   Support my heart to hear thee say:
> "The bird upon its lonely bough
>   Sings sweetest at the close of day." [73]

A glance shows, however, that the selective mind is at work—in "breast" and "brow," and (caught by the same glance) in the aural choice of "movest."

Too much may not easily be said of Landor's variety; too little has ever been said of his depth—unless to doubt it altogether. For felicitous expression of a rare sensibility, we should consider these lines from "Retired this hour from wondering crowds." (He has just reminded Ianthe that romantic ladies do not care for verse that like his is characterized by "lightness, readiness, and ease.") :

> I hate a pomp and a parade
> Of what should ever rest in shade;
> What not the slenderest ray should reach,
> Nor whispered breath of guarded speech:
> There even Memory should sit
> Absorbed, and almost doubting it. [74]

What counts is not the profession but its proof in the last two lines. This is the sensibility that, sorting listeners to music into many who love the art for its own sake, and many who love it because it sets them dreaming, adds,

> Few, when light fingers with sweet voices play
> And melodies swell, pause, and melt away,
> Mind how at every touch, at every tone,
> A spark of life hath glisten'd and hath gone. [75]

Awareness is all. We are physical creatures, and the quality of our thinking is determined by the quality of our senses, which beget thought.

If profundity is the question, we find it in "Lines to a Dragon Fly" which, in its kind, is as profound as Wordsworth. Perhaps it is more so, because it is humorous; because of the lordly carelessness, in his first line, of the literary conventions of cultivated society, and because the hackneyed phrase justifies itself before the end; because of the "stream/Brimful of Moral"—the lazy jest at the word and the deep-hearted appreciation of the fact, both true, and both at once. For humor, being in tune with life and so with eternity, may say and mean two different things in a breath, and in the same sentence be both in and out of earnest. This mood is rare in Landor, and he can afford its rarity; but, if it departed from our civilization, we should find that with it had gone our humanity and our capacity to think.

Lines to a Dragon Fly

Life (priest and poet say) is but a dream;
  I wish no happier one than to be laid
  Beneath some cool syringa's scented shade
Or wavy willow, by the running stream,
  Brimful of Moral, where the Dragon Fly
  Wanders as careless and content as I.
Thanks for this fancy, insect king,
Of purple crest and filmy wing,
Who with indifference givest up
The water-lily's golden cup,
To come again and overlook
What I am writing in my book.
Believe me, most who read the line
Will read with hornier eyes than thine;
And yet their souls shall live for ever,
And thine drop dead into the river!
God pardon them, O insect king,
Who fancy so unjust a thing! [76]

The humor of the poem, the lightness of touch, are integral to the idea, which forbids indignation and a heavy hand, while opening the windows and doors to a mental perspective. Landor has not been admitting the dragon fly to the august company of human beings, but human beings to the expansive company of nature. Not in Wordsworth is there a more perfect and a more grandly gentle evocation of the generosity of life itself and of the freely natural love of living than is in these lines: "Who with indifference givest up/ The water-lily's golden cup. . . ."

V The Nature of His Best in Verse

We may pass over many of Landor's little poems as not marmoreal or memorable, but what should be noticed is that each has a point: the poet always has something to say—an antithesis to make, or some generative likeness to reveal. Often enough the poem as a whole seems hardly more than a vehicle, a preface, or a setting for the main idea; but this appearance is less due to weakness in the whole than to idiosyncratic strength in the part. Most modern poets work mainly by suggestion; they communicate impressions rather than conclusions; their talents are barometric. Mastery of experience is everywhere out of fashion, along with the pleasures of lucidity. In Landor's day such mastery was still admired, though the art of condensation was no less difficult than ever. Doubtless, to perfect any art one must have the gift of whatever temperament it requires; Landor was a sententious man gifted with a rare perceptiveness and with the ear that lucid speech requires. Few writers are capable of such perfect simplicities as "I see, and know not why / Thorns live and roses die." [77]

Lest the idea of sententiousness take up more room here than it deserves, I add that Landor's sense of the phrase is never a prosaic one, and that his verse thoughts require to be thought in verse rather than in prose of whatever memorable kind. To speak of Landor's best, I cite "the dubious apple" in some verses which his Queen Elizabeth (in the imaginary conversation "Queen Elizabeth and Cecil") ascribes to Spenser:

> How much is lost when neither heart nor eye
> Rose-winged Desire or fabling Hope deceives;
> When boyhood with quick throb hath ceased to spy
> The dubious apple in the yellow leaves. . . .[78]

"Rose-winged Desire" and "fabling Hope" rise from a convention of verse, one often the source of delight and utility; something of the word order in these four lines belongs to verse, not to prose; only "the dubious apple" is straight poetry; it has a bold, nonce-phrase quality that in prose would interrupt the progress of a sentence, calling the mind to where it lay darkly gleaming.

Sometimes an idea is all image and melody but as clearly formed as any maxim: "And, tho the grape be plucked away,/Its colour glows amid the leaves." [79] In nearly all his work, the purport steals upon us in an enchantment of music:

> O give me back what Earth, what (without you)
> Not Heaven itself can do—
> One of the golden days that we have past,
> And let it be my last!

> Or else the gift would be, however sweet,
>   Fragile and incomplete.[80]

Although nobody can prove the beauty of a cadence, it may be
worth pointing out, that, of the nine shorter lines in the complete
poem, all but the last begin with an iamb (unless "Not Heaven" is
heard as a spondee). The subtle relief of trochaic "Fragile" and its
invitation to *rubato* are worth experiencing; and the word rings
its idea round with quiet attention.

What but perfection of music preserves "Past ruin'd Ilion," which
graces many a memory, and perhaps as many more anthologies?—
music and the strange charm of the first line, in which time and
place are merged and overcome together.

> Past ruin'd Ilion Helen lives,
>   Alcestis rises from the shades;
> Verse calls them forth; 'tis verse that gives
>   Immortal youth to mortal maids.
>
> Soon shall Oblivion's deepening veil
>   Hide all the peopled hills you see,
> The gay, the proud, while lovers hail
>   In distant ages you and me.
>
> The tear for fading beauty check,
>   For passing glory cease to sigh;
> One form shall rise above the wreck,
>   One name, Ianthe, shall not die.[81]

The poem sings itself, and what it sings is impersonally true, even
to the old boast at the end, which all good poets are entitled to
make. The first two and a half lines have the authority, the splendor,
the Olympian pace of our greatest poetry; the stanza ends with the
present subject set forth in the indestructible balance of perfect
antithesis. It is a satisfaction that "shades" and "maids" seem not
to have been sought for by a rhymer but to have been born for
each other on the page.

The sense of inevitability that comes from the last two stanzas
is arrived at partly by the fact that each advances the idea of the
first, with immortality completing the idea in succeeding sentences;
and that we go, in three steps, from general and impersonal
immortality, to personal but anonymous, and finally to personal
and named—though the very name, in its Classical impersonality,

takes us back to the beginning. Nothing individual or specific in the poem prevents our making every circumstance our own, and that includes, in the imagination of the least of us, the poet's act that immortalizes. The music of this poem is the music to which all elegy aspires. It has demanded not only the ear of a master musician but a mind that is not too possessive—one that, affectionately regarding what it has made, can touch it lightly and let it go.

In a letter to Sidney Colvin, Swinburne said, "In my opinion, the crowning jewel of Landor's minor poems is the quatrain on 'Dirce,' beginning 'Stand close around.' I know of nothing more beautiful (bar Sappho), or perhaps quite so beautiful, in the Anthology." [82]

> Stand close around, ye Stygian set,
>   With Dirce in one boat conveyed!
> Or Charon, seeing, may forget
>   That he is old and she a shade. [83]

Here everything is so compressed, so much the epigrammatical expression of an idea, that the music is more felt than heard. Even so, a reader may be pleasurably conscious of how much the point is both sharpened and strengthened by the "d" sound in its bracing together of "old" and "shade." The beauty of this lyric epitaph is not an accident; it comes, through craftsmanship, from a consciousness that is roving, delicate, and fond of order.

The famous "I strove with none" is another sort of triumph of the antique virtue of restraint:

> I strove with none, for none was worth my strife:
>   Nature I loved, and, next to Nature, Art:
> I warm'd both hands before the fire of Life;
>   It sinks; and I am ready to depart. [84]

As Raleigh said, "Landor has an unerring feeling for impressions that the marble will take." [85] The first line burns like ice, but we must feel it in order to infer the truth of the third. Landor called the quatrain "Dying Speech of an Old Philosopher," and he wrote it on his seventy-fourth birthday. He had many battles still to fight; but it is true that he "warm'd both hands" and that, as a writer, he made no bid for popularity and was nobody's rival.

Some readers cannot hear the quiver of passion in a quiet statement, and they tend to confuse order and control with cruelty and coldness. Landor's eyes were open; the hairs of his flesh responded

to earth's presences, and his whole soul moved with them. In the
nameless quatrain that follows, he might be said to have written his
truest epitaph:

> God scatters beauty as he scatters flowers
> O'er the wide earth, and tells us all are ours.
> A hundred lights in every temple burn,
> And at each shrine I bend my knee in turn.[86]

Is there in that last line a convenient explanation of what people
mean when they call him a minor poet—a first-rate artist in verse,
but a minor figure? This consciousness is not trapped within itself,
and therefore is not of explosive power. The force that Landor
undeniably had expressed itself in physical ways, in fights and feuds,
in strong friendships, in physical exercise, in conversation, and in
the effort of all his writing. Plenty was left for the mind, but he
carelessly, generously scattered it. He seems truly as much interested
in any event of the moment—the budding of a flower, the crowning
of an emperor, a puff of wind, a visit—as major figures seem to be
in the progress of their careers, or in the historical significance of a
velleity so long as it is theirs. Nobody was ever a major figure in
anything he called his amusement; major figures are not relaxed
enough, or fond enough of mere life, or clear-seeing and humble
enough to smile at what they take seriously; or, if they pass this
test of littleness, they must at least have leaned enough, and hard
and long enough, in one direction for us to feel their weight. "And
at each shrine I bend my knee in turn" is not—in its gift of attention, and its dispersal of powers—the way to be great; but it may be
a way to be good, wise, and beautiful.

It is important to thank a poet for what he has given us, and
enough may not have been said even yet of the variety of Landor's
poetry and the quality of his best work. "Faesulan Idyl" (*Faesulae*
is the old Latin form of *Fiesole*) may help to summarize what that
work offers us.

> Here, where precipitate Spring with one light bound
> Into hot Summer's lusty arms expires;
> And where go forth at morn, at eve, at night,
> Soft airs, that want the lute to play with them,
> And softer sighs, that know not what they want;
> Under a wall, beneath an orange-tree
> Whose tallest flowers could tell the lowlier ones
> Of sights in Fiesole right up above,

While I was gazing a few paces off
At what they seemed to show me with their nods,
Their frequent whispers and their pointing shoots,
A gentle maid came down the garden steps
And gathered the pure treasure in her lap.
I heard the branches rustle, and stept forth
To drive the ox away, or mule, or goat,
(Such I believed it must be); for sweet scents
Are the swift vehicles of stil sweeter thoughts,
And nurse and pillow the dull memory
That would let drop without them her best stores.
They bring me tales of youth and tones of love,
And 'tis and ever was my wish and way
To let all flowers live freely, and all die,
Whene'er their Genius bids their souls depart,
Among their kindred in their native place.
I never pluck the rose; the violet's head
Hath shaken with my breath upon its bank
And not reproacht me; the ever-sacred cup
Of the pure lily hath between my hands
Felt safe, unsoil'd, nor lost one grain of gold.
I saw the light that made the glossy leaves
More glossy; the fair arm, the fairer cheek
Warmed by the eye intent on its pursuit;
I saw the foot, that, altho half-erect
From its grey slipper, could not lift her up
To what she wanted: I held down a branch
And gather'd her some blossoms, since their hour
Was come, and bees had wounded them, and flies
Of harder wing were working their way thro
And scattering them in fragments under foot.
So crisp were some, they rattled unevolved,
Others, ere broken off, fell into shells,
For such appear the petals when detacht,
Unbending, brittle, lucid, white like snow,
And like snow not seen thro, by eye or sun:
Yet every one her gown received from me
Was fairer than the first. . I thought not so,
But so she praised them to reward my care.
I said: *you find the largest.*

> *This indeed,*

Cried she, *is large and sweet.*

> She held one forth,

Whether for me to look at or to take

> She knew not, nor did I; but taking it
> Would best have solved (and this she felt) her doubts.
> I dared not touch it; for it seemed a part
> Of her own self; fresh, full, the most mature
> Of blossoms, yet a blossom; with a touch
> To fall, and yet unfallen.
>
> > > > > > > She drew back
> The boon she tendered, and then, finding not
> The ribbon at her waist to fix it in,
> Dropt it, as loth to drop it, on the rest.[87]

The idyl develops with a Wordsworthian leisureliness and with a fond, evocative attention to intimate detail that may properly be regarded as Landor's own. The mood is exquisitely balanced, like a blossom on the fingertips, from its first announcement to the end. There was in Landor, as in some other men, a responsiveness that knew how close an approach certain subjects could bear: he could sense their withdrawal. He knew that essences are not to be handled, that atmosphere cannot be duplicated, that poetry cannot be paraphrased.

What in "Faesulan Idyl" can we point out in our mere prose? The season, a moment between full bloom and the setting of the fruit; soft airs and sighs, hesitancies and motions toward fulfillment; the rare experience of what has grown freely to astral perfectness, before the change to another kind of beauty—things that, as Shakespeare knew, "Hold in perfection but a little moment"; herself, ". . . fresh, full, the most mature/Of blossoms, yet a blossom; with a touch/To fall, and yet unfallen." Then her blind movement to fix the branch at her waist, and her light slow dropping of it, with all its blossoms, on the rest.

In this unspoken intercourse of souls is revealed the dramatic power that Browning recognized in Landor and, above all, the *knowledge* that comes before poetry as before wisdom. What loving observation preceded that pose in which the foot "altho half-erect/From its grey slipper, could not lift her up/To what she wanted." That the poet had, as it were, perched on blossoming boughs is evident in the extraordinarily fine detail. Bees, he says, had wounded the blossoms—and we begin to feel intimately that sweetness attracts the spoiler, that the time of bloom is passing, and that what is perfect must now be looked for in the fruit. Bees and flies are not so much agents as signs of the season, and our sense of reality in the whole arises from the minute observation, which becomes our own experience: "Flies of harder wing"! And experienced, however inexpressibly, is the opaque and secretive lucidity of maiden white.

This poem is a rarity, though its virtues and the earthliness of its harmony are all Landor's. It is not—it could not be—epigrammatic: its strokes are those of a wand. Yet the last fifteen lines are as homely as Robert Frost; they are also less self-conscious and more exquisite. The naturalness of the style is a grace of mind; it is elegant, like the patterns of achievement in nature herself.

CHAPTER 4

Prose: The Form Chosen

I A Substitute for Play and Novel?

S IR Philip Sidney, speaking here in an imaginary conversation with Lord Brooke, might be Landor speaking for himself:

So little am I ashamed of the hours I spend in poetry, even a consciousness that the poetry itself is bad never leads me to think the occupation is. Foliage, herbage, pebbles, may put in motion the finer parts of the mind; and although the first things it throws off be verses, and indifferent ones, we are not to despise the cultivator of them, but to consider him as possessing the garden of innocence, at which the great body of mankind looks only through the gate.

In the corner formed by the court-wall, sheltered and sunny, I found, earlier in the season than usual, a little rose-bud; which perhaps owed its existence to my cutting the plant in summer, when it began to intrude on the path, and had wetted the legs of the ladies with the rain it held. None but trifling poetry could be made out of this, yet other than trifling pleasure was.

A trifle in verse from Landor may be perfect, and thus unrivaled; something ambitious, in the realms where perfection is unknown, makes every man a challenger. Landor preferred not to be fatuous; he knew his powers and would not be content without having done something of noble note. He continued to write dramatic verse, along with the other forms, because he was a maker; but, for his pride and his genius, he found, as he wrote to Browning, "more room" in prose. Moreover, he observed that "We had no prose-writer interesting in his subject and graceful in his style. We had none who could stand with Pascal, De Sevigne, Bossuet and Le Sage—nor do I think the Romans had, or even the Greeks." [1] He made a place for himself, a peculiarly French sort of place in English literature, as a classic artist in prose. In France, such names are revered; they even have historical influence, like Cognac or Roquefort.

If prose was Landor's study and business, it also was a lifelong and sustaining amusement. Not everyone would say that his miscellaneous performances—mostly political, like *To the Burgesses of Warwick* (1797) or *Commentary on Memoirs of Mr. Fox* (1812); some literary, like the essay on Catullus—are the work of a greatly gifted writer; but Carlyle admired his essay "Francesco Petrarca," and Mr. Super calls it the jewel of Landor's writings.[2] Landor, like almost any other man, did his best work within bounds; and the discipline of verse gave the poet his freedom. When he was set at liberty, like Montaigne, to say in prose whatever occurred to him, his force was dissipated; his genius, the relation-finding faculty, undeclared. The practical, pagan, home-keeping equanimity of Montaigne was in itself enough to give a frame and a direction to his essays; Landor, wholehearted, idealistic, thin-skinned, irascible, and thirsting for quiet, must begin his work within some convention of order. He once said to William Macready, the famous actor-manager—and he must have been thinking not only of his plays— that "I have not the constructive faculty. I can only set persons talking; all the rest is chance."[3] What he called "chance," if these are his exact words, was the working of an inquisitive and experienced mind and sensibility within the bounds of character and situation, from moment to moment as a life or a thought grows, and not from end to beginning in justification of a superimposed plan. If he was to work in prose, all he needed was something in the way of bounds or regulations; then, on a road of some kind, pointed in an actual direction, he would be free to go his own way and think in an orderly fashion. This order is what the dialogue offered Landor—and he experimented with it for years before he made it his chosen form. In the first place, it *was* a form; it required a self-discipline that the essay did not, while offering an endless range of thoughts to think, songs to sing, and characters to create. It offered the satisfaction of philosophy and the glory of drama.

Landor was at pains to remind his readers—and the reminder is necessary—that the form needed no apology: "The better parts of Homer are in dialogue: and downward from him to Galileo

the noblest works of human genius have assumed this form: among
the rest I am sorry to find no few heretics and scoffers. At the
present day the fashion is over: every man pushes every other
man behind him, and will let none speak out but himself." [4]

Landor's imaginary Quinctus Cicero is of the opinion that "the
best oration can only show the clever man, while Philosophy shows
the great one." And Marcus Tullius replies: "I approve of the
Dialogue for the reason you have given me just now: the fewness
of settled truths, and the facility of turning the cycle of our thoughts
to what aspect we wish, as geometers and astronomers the globe." [5]

Landor's desire to express his own thoughts on all subjects
could hardly be questioned by anyone who has come within range
of his voice; the suggestion of sympathetic interest in the other side
of a question, however, may be a little humanly disingenuous. More
conscientiously systematic writers of dialogue than Landor have
been as loyally wedded to their own thoughts as he and less desirous
of bringing all their speakers alive. The poet in Landor is a kind
of providence, affirming the worth of life; it fosters the little flame
in all his speakers as he leads them by the hand into our presence.

The miscellaneity, the happy inclusiveness of his work in verse,
which is that of a man for whom all that is and happens in life
is a family matter, informs Landor's prose as well. He is not above
striking a formal attitude in public—in dedications and prefaces,
for instance—when he seems suddenly aware of standing up in
front of everybody; and, in introducing his first two volumes of
Imaginary Conversations of Literary Men and Statesmen (1824),
he declares: "I hope to leave behind me completed the great object
of my studies, an orderly and solid work in history." [6]

A preface five years later (to the *Second Series* of *Imaginary
Conversations*) says, with gloom and constraint, that he had once
projected conversations, ancient and modern, that should discuss
"the systems of ethics, the varieties of style, the defects and ex-
cellencies of poetry and poets" and that "traces of this design" are
to be discovered in the five volumes thus far published. [7] Much truer
to the spirit of all his life and work was his refusal to allow Forster
to omit most of the political dialogues from the collected edition of
1846, because without the Ferdinands and Don John Marys (kings
of Spain and Portugal), the book would cease "to represent all the
parts of life which I propose to exhibit in it." [8] This Landor is the
one who, in August, 1847, wrote to Forster of his Latin Idyls:

"You shall say, and not only as a friend but as a Critic, that no other man, not even the great and glorious Callimachus, has written with more variety. This is all I lay claim to." [9]

The boy Landor who called his *Gebir* a poem "descriptive of men and manners" [10] is later the man of seventy who wrote to Forster: "My Conversations, whatever their demerits, will exhibit more qualities and postures of the human mind than any other book published in my day. Above two hundred men and women will live again; and, among the rest, neither Cicero nor Solon will be proved to have spoken more eloquently or more wisely in his former state." [11] The conversations convey a sense of varied life and of many thousands of thoughts. Landor's view of himself as historian is almost exactly that of Fielding; both are poets, aiming at the beauty of truth.

Dialogue is not only a vehicle of ideas for Landor; it might also be considered as a substitute for the play or the novel, a substitute free of their difficulties of construction. In character, which he called "the business of the dialogue," [12] and in the life of ideas, he could satisfy his need to express the drama of things: their inter-action, their relative positions, their light and shade—all that makes us conscious of existence.

II *Action and Character*

Forster's arrangement of the conversations into Classical Dialogues, Dialogues of Sovereigns and Statesmen, of Literary Men, of Famous Women, and Miscellaneous Dialogues is both convenient and reasonable. But a different kind of classification from Forster's has asserted itself in the passage of time; editors who hoped to attract readers to a volume of selections have tended to draw heavily upon the more "dramatic" dialogues.

Some of the dialogues are obvious dramatic-action pieces, none more exclusively than "Rhadamistus and Zenobia," which is two or three minutes of hectic speech in the midst of flight, at the climax of which Rhadamistus, to save his wife from the enemy, strikes her with his sword and throws her into the Araxes. Character does have time to emerge; and action in so literal a sense is rare in dialogue. What is more normal in the dialogues is emotional action, or dramatic movement of the feelings, with death or danger at our side. A highly charged example is "The Empress Catharine and

Princess Dashkof," in which Peter III is murdered by Catharine's command on the other side of the double door, while the murderess chats and sweats. ("It is unnecessary to inform the generality of readers," says Landor in a note in the first edition, "that Catharine was not present at the murder of her husband; nor is it easy to believe that Clytemnestra was at the murder of hers. Our business is character.")

"Marcellus and Hannibal" is the meeting, not of enemies, but of two heroes; it lasts the short time Marcellus takes to die, and its elegiac language is filled with the strange tender selflessness of which we are sure great blood-letters are capable. In "Tiberius and Vipsania," the former has not recovered from their politically ordered divorce. Under his deep feeling for Vipsania we find the guilt and despair of a lover for whom his own ambition and the wills of others were too strong; and, as his speech grows more violent, we feel, and understand that Vipsania does too, the slow surge of madness in Tiberius. "O cease, my sweet Tiberius! Stamp not upon that stone: my heart lies under it."

In 1830, Crabb Robinson noted that "People do not talk as Landor supposes." [13] People do not talk as Landor *enables* them to do. The convention he is following is that of verse drama—of the drama, in other words—in which the novel itself grew great. The less the conventions of literary speech allow us to tinker with language, the less chance our literature has of interesting anyone next month.

"Richard I and the Abbot of Boxley," which makes more use of narrative, is so much more nearly complete as an incident that it might easily be staged. The abbot finds his beloved king undefeated though a captive, and Richard's words of strength and courage are finely highlighted with evidences of more than heroic character:

I debark in Sicily, place my hand upon the throne of Tancred, and fix it. Again we sail, and within a day or two, behold! as the sun is setting, the solitary majesty of Crete, mother of a religion, it is said, that lived two thousand years. Onward, and many bright specks bubble up along the blue Aegean; islands, every one of which, if the songs and stories of the pilots are true, is the monument of a greater man than I am. We leave them afar off—and for whom? For creatures of less import than the sea-mews on their cliffs. . . . [14]

Hofer, the Tyrolean rebel in "Andrew Hofer, Count Metternich, and the Emperor Francis," is everybody's dramatic hero who throws his life away for the pleasure of saying what he pleases to the "great." We understand, meanwhile, that they are the slaves of greater power; he, the free man. This dialogue is prevented from being a study of character by the automatic sympathy and excitement it generates and by the fact that the author approves of them. Landor had no intention of saying a good word for coldness of heart and political expediency (has a decent author ever cared for Metternich?) or of deprecating idealism, self-abnegation, and the taste for simple pleasures. It remains to be said that no expectation is disappointed and that the writing is full of zest.

A subtler scene is found in "William Wallace and King Edward I," in which Edward is half-seduced by admiration for his incorruptible prisoner. The interest is in the force one character exerts upon another. An equally simple situation to begin with, but made round, complete, and many-faceted, is that of "Alexander and the Priest of Hammon," in which we see the conqueror bullied. Alexander, in his role as Son of Jupiter Ammon, deigns to visit his father's shrine in order to exact a declaration of his divinity. The young man, trying to bluster only in the casual way of the supremely great, is from the beginning at the mercy of the deeply experienced, fearless, and witty priest. The priest maneuvers him into agreeing, as ritual demands, to marry his goddess sister—who, of course, turns out to be a great snake, more devoutly called "dragon." Landor's resolution of this comedy is beautifully sure in every touch—hilarious, cynical, strong, gentle, and wise.

This dialogue is in so many ways one of action that we might think of it as easily staged. But how crude the following gesture would be if acted out, so as to leave no words necessary but some short "What's the matter?"

Priest. . . . Son Alexander, art thou not satisfied? What ails thee, drawing the back of thy hand across thine eyes?

Alexander. A little dust flew into them as the door opened.

Priest. Of that dust are the sands of the desert and the kings of Macedon.[15]

This is pure dialogue, for the gestures are contained in what the speakers say; it is also literature written to be read, with pastures of experience to browse in between the lines.

III   *The Drama of Character*

In many of the dialogues, concentration upon character itself is specifically dramatic. In them, we might say, we find a substitute for the novel rather than for the play. In "King James I and Isaac Casaubon" what matters is not the theological discussion but what most clearly emerges from it: the highly colored yet chill and pinched vivacity of James. "Louis XVIII and Talleyrand" is the picture of a king with just enough intelligence to cause Talleyrand to stop for a moment, now and then, in his dancing of mental rings around him. Landor allows Louis to wake up quietly, in the end, and to put Talleyrand in his place on two scores: the misuse of supreme power, and the mere habit of diplomatic flattery. The reader enjoys the triumph of simplicity without any aid from the sentimental.

Another reversal of what we expect of a character as it has craftily been revealed comes in "Lord Bacon and Richard Hooker." Bacon, in disgrace, sighs at the thought of what the nation is coming to: he thinks the use of a silver work a "monstrous sign of voluptuousness"; he berates a servant for bringing in Malmsey, which he has reserved for himself as a medicine. He is showing some of the infirmities and follies of which, he says, the well informed and the ill informed have "nearly the same quantity." Then, at the climax of a summary of his points of intellectual greatness, he remarks that one subject of "useful and rational inquiry" has almost escaped him—Francis Bacon.[16] The reader may balance between two impressions: that Bacon is incorrigibly superior, and that Landor has forced a comment in edgewise.

"What an imagination is Bacon's; what splendid and ardent language!"[17] exclaims Isaac Barrow, in the imaginary conversation between Barrow and Isaac Newton; it is part of a long critical discussion of Bacon and of much else of importance in the cultivation of minds. From Barrow comes advice on scholarly life, style, friendship, and marriage. The ideas of the two do not clash but draw out and support one another as, gradually, the portraits are developed—of an older and a younger man; of fatherly friendship and filial affection and dependence; of a strong and distinguished mind quite capable of turning over his professorship at an early age to the boy whose genius he recognized, cherished, and did not flatter; and of a Newton youthful, naïve, tentative. What is moving about this dialogue is its truth to the relationship: the passing of experience down from mind to mind; the patience, the restraint; and the touch of sadness—of infinite distances between minds.

At the other end of the gamut is a dialogue in which the interest in character has little to do with intellect. In the circumstances of Beniowski, a captive Pole (once not only a soldier but a man of rank) who has fallen in love with his pupil—the consequent wild admonitions to "Fly!"; the imagined hardships together, wolves and bears, cannibalism, and watery graves—we find blooming the sweet, ignorant, loving loyalty of the pupil, Aphanasia. Kotzebue wrote a play on Beniowski; Landor's four pages on Aphanasia amount to nothing.[18]

Of Landor's dialogues on characters in danger, as memorable as any is "Henry VIII and Anne Boleyn," which depicts a conversation on the eve of Anne's beheading. It is not so full and varied a view of Anne as the verse scene (page 41 above) between her and the Constable of the Tower, in part because there is no limit to what we may learn by poetry and in part because the presence here of Henry is a somewhat confining one. Yet in the prose scene there is room for Anne's spirited, happy nature. There is time for her to change from wife to heroic woman and then, a moment later, to be drawn back by nature and habit to wife again but without the intimacy there was before.

Anne. O my dear husband! it must be a naughty thing, indeed, that makes him angry beyond remission. Did you ever try how pleasant it is to forgive anyone? There is nothing else wherein we can resemble God perfectly and easily.

Henry. Resemble God perfectly and easily! Do vile creatures talk thus of the Creator?

Anne. No, Henry, when his creatures talk thus of him, they are no longer vile creatures! When they know that he is good, they love him; and, when they love him, they are good themselves. O Henry! my husband and King! the judgments of our Heavenly Father are righteous: on this, surely, we must think alike.

Henry. And what, then? Speak out: again I command thee, speak plainly! thy tongue was not so torpid but this moment. Art ready? Must I wait?

Anne. If any doubt remains upon your royal mind of your equity in this business; should it haply seem possible to you that passion or prejudice, in yourself or another, may have warped so strong an understanding,—do but supplicate the Almighty to strengthen and enlighten it, and he will hear you.

Henry. What! thou wouldst fain change thy quarters, ay?

Anne. My spirit is detached and ready, and I shall change them shortly, whatever your Highness may determine.[19]

And she now dreams aloud of her native Bickling, its fruit trees,

and the gorse on the hill; and, as if with her head back and her
eyes half open upon a husband incapable of sharing her thoughts,
but one in no way dangerous, she teases him with the question
"May I go back to it?" Still communing with herself, she thanks
him for having planted his park at Greenwich after her childish
notion, "tree for tree, the very same as at Bickling." His reply—
"Silly child! as if thou shouldst see them any more"—is infantile
in its barbarity. She remains the better poet of the two; and, before
becoming all mother at the end, she can refresh herself with a dip
into irony.[20]

In "The Maid of Orleans and Agnes Sorel" the emphasis is
indeed character: a dramatic confrontation of, and crisis in, character. In the beginning, Agnes is charmed with the boy-girl, impressed with her as the conqueror, and amused at the devout and
awkward rustic. Step by step, however, she is caught by the saintli-
ness of Jeanne, bound tight in her own sense of sin, and persuaded,
in the heat of conversion, to drive the King from her side into
battle. One of the first things we learn about Jeanne is that she has
known what it is to be afraid—of the lowing of a young steer, of
the butting of a full-grown kid, of the barking of a house dog at his
gate, and finally:

I scarcely dared kiss the child, when he called on me with burning
tongue in the pestilence of a fever.
   Agnes. No wonder! A creature in a fever! what a frightful thing!
   Jeanne. It would be, were it not so piteous.
   Agnes. And did you kiss it? Did you really kiss the lips?
   Jeanne. I fancied mine would refresh them a little.
   Agnes. And did they? I should have thought mine could do but
trifling good in such cases.[21]

This quality revealed in Agnes is what is to be overcome—a lifetime of fastidiousness, of decorative sophistication, of worship of
loveliness; and, poor clear-seeing and kindly creature, her love of
Charles: "Bid him leave me! wish it! permit it! think it near! believe
it ever can be! Go, go.—I am lost eternally." [22] But Agnes is saved
by the blessed Jeanne from the divinity of love for the unhappiness
and the privilege of rescuing France.

The portraiture has been done by the skill of Landor, and by
no other means: the kiss in pestilence, the contrast in lips and
kinds of love, the risk of burning, the radiance of simplicity. Such
an imaginary conversation is not a substitute but a legitimate

fictional form. If all the dialogues were on the order of this one and if the form were wholly consigned to the subject of character, we should have had to do without the richness of the greatest ones, which have a burden of thought.

An important aspect of character in the work of Landor is that it leads to fun. "Bossuet and the Duchess de Fontanges" is comedy and its own excuse for being. Bossuet himself does not sound much like anyone but a great churchman and writer forced to be the new confessor, in a comedy, to Madame de Fontanges, who has just been made a duchess for having greatly pleased King Louis. Little Fontanges is the treasure of the piece, as well as all that makes it go: she is seventeen and without a thought in her head. All honor to the men who established that tradition of comedy according to which a stupid woman may charm us into heaven! Only one of the *sottises* of Fontanges is much labored, and that is her confusion of Quietism with sleepiness in church. She talks so fast, however, that it is easy to forget—and Landor easy to forgive. She never does think of anything to confess to Father Bossuet. Nor, when informed that "we must detest our bodies, if we would save our souls," can she see anything detestable in hers. At any rate, it is easier to love. "I love God," she says, "whenever I think of him, he has been so very good to me." [23]

"Peter the Great and Alexis" is not comedy of manners, but its virtues are comic. In it the contrast of characters is of first importance; without it, Peter would not shine. Strictly speaking, Peter would not make the most agreeable of dinner companions, but in this dialogue he is delightful. The delight is called forth by language and the way it moves; the mind can hardly deny a place to such vigor. Alexis, haled home from Austria, to which he had fled, is a disappointment to his father in wisdom, duty, spirit, courage, and ambition: "I have educated thee among my guards and horses, among my drums and trumpets, among my flags and masts." Not all readers deserve such a sentence, crowned as it is with that last phrase so full of breeze and upward look, and echoing with a crowded life swept clear and clean with freedom and work and the joys of defiance. Peter takes another breath:

When thou wert a child, and couldst hardly walk, I have taken thee into the arsenal, though children should not enter according to regulations; I have there rolled cannon-balls before thee over iron plates; and I have shown thee bright new arms, bayonets and sabres; and I have pricked the back of my hands until the blood came out in many places; and I have made thee lick it; and I have then done the same to thine. Afterward, from thy tenth year, I have mixed gunpowder in thy grog; I have peppered thy peaches; I have poured bilge-water (with a little good wholesome tar in it) upon thy melons; I have brought out girls to mock thee and cocker thee, and talk like mariners, to make thee braver. Nothing would do.

At one moment we might think of Caliban and of the wide-open eyes and appetite for life that deny the brute and bind us to him. Next we might wonder how such a speech as Peter's can escape our derision. If we paraphrase it, the so-called substance of what he says is both asinine and intolerable. If then we read it once more as it is written, the substance is something else: hopeful crassness happily working against nature. This is the kind of humor that rings in the halls of Olympus; it is joy of life, crackling and shining as when English was lived, not merely written. "I have peppered thy peaches!" The man who is not made happier by that does not know what life and poetry can be. Peter continues, with a father's pride in himself: "Nay, recollect thee! I have myself led thee forth to the window when fellows were hanged and shot; and have shown thee every day the halves and quarters of bodies; and I have sent an orderly or chamberlain for the heads; and I have pulled the cap up from over the eyes; and I have made thee, in spite of thee, look steadfastly upon them, incorrigible coward!" [24]

In this speech, the fun flags, and it is meant to; but it is hard not to regard Alexis, when he speaks, as a poor thing, and to feel that there is something too nasally perfect about his sentiments. Landor's Alexis loves his father and, before he can be executed, dies of a broken heart not only because he is not loved in return (though Peter once shows kindness) but, as Forster suggests, because he is unable to be what his father requires. [25]

Strictly speaking, again, this dialogue is, in its purpose, pathetic fiction; but it has become something else because of Landor's enthusiasm for the histrionic attractions of his idea of Peter the Great. When Peter, grown incoherent in his desire to make philosophical and moral sense, calls his son "Mr. Professor," are we supposed to stand against him? [26] Are we to shake our heads and cluck when he objects to having been told of his son's death just before dinner? What are we to do but dine with him, on the instant, when he calls for a bottle of brandy and "a rasher of bacon on thy life! and some pickled sturgeon, and some krout and caviar, and good strong cheese." [27] So the dialogue ends. This is not Old King Cole but the maker of a nation, who can shout like the Old Testament: "Have I not shaved my people, and breeched them?" [28]

"Louis XIV and Father LaChaise" is more simply a farce arising from something disproportionate. Louis is about to confess to having "committed an action" during his Dutch wars, but he takes some time to do so. Meanwhile, he has described the state of the Dutch with a heartlessness that would in itself be enough to confess to for one lifetime—but then, as he says, God had thus punished Dutch heresy. He had acted as God's agent by bribing the favorite dissolute sons of prominent families, getting them drunk, and converting them. Thus far, the farce is heavy satire. It improves as it takes on a happy extravagance, not only in the delineation of character, but in the words themselves—and as it gradually approaches the action that must be confessed:

Intelligence was brought to me that the cook of the English general had prepared a superb dinner, in consequence of what that insolent and vainglorious people are in the habit of calling a success. "We shall soon see," exclaimed I, "who is successful: God protects France." The whole army shouted, and, I verily believe, at that moment would have conquered the world. I deferred it: my designs lie in my own breast. Father, I never heard such a shout in my life: it reminded me of Cherubim and Seraphim and Archangels. The infantry cried with joy, the horses capered and neighed and ventriloquized right and left, from an excess of animation. Leopard skins, bear-skins, Genoa velvet, Mechlin ruffles, Brussels cravats, feathers and fringes and golden bands, up in the air at once; pawings and snortings, threats and adjurations, beginnings and ends of songs. I was Henry and Caesar, Alexander and David, Charlemagne and Agamemnon. . . .[29]

It is a festival of language. Imperceptibly, we draw closer to confession. His men had intercepted a letter from the wife of the English general, telling her husband that to celebrate his victory she was sending him "a glorious *mince-pie*": " 'Devil incarnate!' said I, on reading the despatch, 'I will disappoint thy malice.' I was so enraged that I went within a mile or two of cannon-shot. . . ." [30] He captured the pie and ate it—on a Friday. Understandably enough, he lost battles and the pie sat uneasily. The penance now proposed by Father LaChaise is to limit his majesty to three kinds of wine and three of liqueurs, and oysters of Cancale are to be

eaten raw from the barrel or scalloped or both. After a short dis-
quisition on the program of events to come on the Last Day, the
conversation ends on the theological position of quail; and LaChaise
comments: "There are naturalists who assert that quails have fallen
from heaven like manna. Externally, they bear the appearance of
birds, and I have eaten them in that persuasion. . . ." [31]

When the interest is mainly satire, character is distorted, though
it will not necessarily be weakened or be undramatic. In the dialogue
just described, satire holds little more than its normal place in
comedy; the passages on the penance have a comic inevitability
about them rather than the mordancy of an attack on the institution;
and the quotation about quail is, as wit, almost art for art's sake.

Landor's "Soliman and Mufti" is downright oafish in spots ("are
we in the mosque? that thou utterest these idle fancies—truths I
mean" [32]) because satire of what is foreign to us is both easy and
completely impossible. When the foreign (Islam) is, however, a
means of satirizing the domestic (Catholicism), the result is rather
better. For instance, the immovable Mufti advises that the Koran be
kept from contamination by the hands of the public and "that it
be served out to them decorously and ceremoniously, like sher-
bet." [33] Soliman, who has ordered (and this is his role in the
dialogue) that the book be translated into all languages, is less
interesting than the Mufti; and, after countermanding his order, he
is sent on his way by Landor to the bath, the harem, and a consign-
ment of promising Georgians. He has, however, been allowed to
join with the Mufti in enunciating a little lesson in statecraft, which
we shall call "The Plough and the Harrow":

Soliman. My resolution is to scatter the good seed in all lands, having
now well ploughed and harrowed them.
Mufti. Suppose, O my master and lord! we turn the plough and
harrow over them another time or two.
Soliman. God is merciful! we cannot do that, if they embrace the
faith. [34]

Character used for satiric purposes may be limited either by
underemphasis and underdevelopment or by overemphasis and
underdevelopment. The first kind may be found in the general
satire "Emperor of China and Tsing-Ti"; the second, in a number
of personal and topical efforts. The Chinese dialogue, divided into
eight "audiences" with the Emperor, is a feeble descendant of such
eighteenth-century efforts as Montesquieu's *Persian Letters* and

Goldsmith's *Citizen of the World*. Though long enough to make a considerable place for itself in the genre, this dialogue has nothing of the breadth and depth we would hope for; it is little more than a languid, verbose commentary on the working of Christianity as compared with its principles. How do the English manage to be known as Christians when they have wholly rejected Christianity? Much of the information brought back to the Emperor is satirical of Christian history, particularly of everything since Trinitarianism, which strikes the Chinese as an odd sort of accounting; the Catholic refusal of Christian burial rites to people who have done so much as actors have to make us happy is as shocking to Chinese intelligence as the concept of punishment by everlasting fire. The Emperor is a complete humanitarian as well as a man of some worldly experience: "Let every man choose his idol as freely as he chooses his wife; let him be constant if he can; if he can not, let him at least be civil." [35]

A ray of light in the European Darkness is a Whig note evidently with regard to Catholic Emancipation, which is read to the Emperor by Tsing-Ti: "Hold nothing back from any man that is his, and least of all urge as a reason for it that you hold it back now because you have been holding it back many years." [36] Related to this is one of the too-few roving comments on English society: that the English avoid the trouble of reforming any abuse by the armor-clad observation that "This is not the time." [37]

This dialogue is worth reading, but it is not so brilliant as some in which Landor has been able to turn from subject to subject and mood to mood as one led to or uncovered another. It is not so much that he lacks the "constructive" faculty as that he does not want it, for it forces him to stay in one spot; and his mind does not naturally dredge, it browses. Even to take a satiric point of view for a given length of time deadens his spirit; he must have his freedom.

Topical satire is a death trap for any artist; probably no more than ten years after the production of the first work of art, the virtues of universality were once for all discovered. Nevertheless, our responses to life continue to be personal and immediate, and we relieve our minds with no thought of the morrow and the need for footnotes, or of the vast and ponderous apathy of the world. As satire becomes more personal, more pointed, the characters lose every charm but what they may gain as excellent examples of the art of caricature. King Ferdinand VII of Spain, Landor's contemporary, in "Don Victor Saez and El Rey Netto," is a convenient illustration of the rule:

Rey Netto. . . . Heretics are very stubborn: Fire alone can soften and bend them. At present we are able but to treat them as ferrets, and sew their mouths up. On this achievement the sons of Saint Louis are unanimously resolved.

Saez. Faith, hope, and charity are resplendent on your Majesty's countenance, whose gracious smiles, like beams from heaven, announce the certain accomplishment of your pious wishes.

Rey Netto. I did not smile about sewing up their mouths like ferrets; but—upon my life I cannot help laughing—do you think it practicable? They must be careful in binding well both arms and feet. Now, my dear father Don Victor, as there should always be some person to seize the legs of the criminal who is hanged, could not I be so disguised as to perform the office, and nobody know it? The hand of a man who dies by the halter is a cure for some diseases; a mere touch effects it. The leg of Riego, pulled as I should pull it, would to me be a panacea like the milk of St. Catharine's neck or the oil running from her body.[38]

The trouble with this as literature is that the author is not master of his feelings. No doubt there are men on the earth who behave like monsters; but in order for us to feel the truth of the fact more strongly than the shiver it causes, the mind of the artist must be at a cool remove, so that he himself is fuller of understanding than of excitement or revulsion. Truth is less personal than what Landor gives us here; being by definition what abides, it must be sought for deeper down and with a farther-ranging eye, a more comprehensive reach of imagination. We might recall that triumph of satire in *Candide,* when our young victim of the Inquisition is beaten on the posteriors in time with the anthem. Let that stand, as Sterne might say, for a whole sermon upon the subject.

Yet there is more to be said on it. In becoming personal, satire loses the humor that is its hold on truth; for the same reasons the same thing happens when satire becomes propaganda. We may write off several of Landor's dialogues that are little more than pamphleteering; among these are "Marshal Bugeaud and Arab Chieftain," "Nicholas, Frederick-William, Nesselrode," and, in fact, most of the dialogues found at the end of the sixth volume of Crump's edition. Perhaps the most unpleasantly striking of these failures is "Queen Pomare, Pritchard, Captains Polverel and Des Mitrailles, Lieut. Poignaunez, Mariners," in which Landor takes advantage of a report of vicious mistreatment of the queen of Tahiti to give free rein to his dislike of the French.

If what Landor tells us is historical fact, the human truth of savagery has been blurred beyond our capacity for rational judgment by the heated partisanship of his version. In the end, all such representations suffer from the passion that informs them; they draw us down into the maelstrom, where we become entangled with the Enemy and lost. Landor was hotly in touch with life at many points; if he had not been, he could not so often have written wisely and well. No writer can be more than a man, but these human weaknesses are deadly ones.

Such dialogues, along with the political dialogues in general, are not uninteresting; and though, as Landor said, they add to the variety of the population, the man of a later century is likely not to find much in them that is addressed to him. The situation is different when, as in most of his work, we may join Landor and his diverse companions as contemporaries, speaking at ease the common language, which has lasted.

IV *Narrative as an Intrusive Force*

Two conversations ought to be briefly discussed as examples of what happens when Landor is as much interested in narrative as in character. In these instances, dialogue is patently an excuse—a means of indulging in some of the pleasures of fiction while ignoring the technical problems it poses. "Duke de Richelieu, Sir Firebrace Cotes, Lady Glengrin, and Mr. Normanby," which covers ninety-two pages of fairly small print in the Crump edition, aspires left-handedly to be a novella. It has its own narrator and commentator, as a novel has the right to do, who takes the characters by sea from Nice to Dublin and to the Irish countryside. Meanwhile, for the benefit of the main character, that Duke of Richelieu who had much to do with the founding of modern Odessa (here traveling as Colonel Le Doux), Mr. Normanby tells his own story, and he is followed by one or two others of shorter wind. In the end, our statesman has belatedly been allowed to learn the political value of happiness, but that fact has nothing to do with the rest of the piece—if so flagrantly miscellaneous a series of chance accretions could merit the name.

Normanby himself is a fine fellow, muscular, thoughtful, responsible, and devout. Stylistically, he is able to cope with the diversity of types about which he reports; he is not, however, the man to tell a farcical tale about a hasty marriage. Landor has simply forced Normanby into this employment, thereby splitting his character down the middle. The other characters named in the title are ghostly or, like Le Doux, absorptive.

This dialogue, if that is what it ought to be called, is a collection of small episodes of a sort familiar enough to readers of the old novels—a domestic idyl, the mistakes of a night at an inn, a visit to a great man (Thomas Paine), the effects of a legacy. It is bright, varied, and vivacious. It displays, however, the great flaw of Landor's particularly narrative dialogues: failure in emphasis. Persons and plots are introduced and sketchily carried forward by casual references. If the reader nods, he will lose track of everything; for the narrative proceeds by digression, and what on one page was the story of the son is on the next the story of the father, or of the doctor who got the father his bride. Yet Landor's awkwardness in certain technical matters seems not only unimportant and unmemorable but somehow disconnected from himself; for his air is not that of a man capable of failure. He is one of the few *grands seigneurs* in English literature.

Although there are admirable passages of a rough but amiable vigor of the Smollett and Dickens kind, samples of the best this dialogue offers would probably be in a serious vein—as is this expanded aphorism: "The habit of haranguing is in itself pernicious: I have known even the conscientious and pious, the humane and liberal, dried up by it, and have watched the mind growing black and rancid in its own smoke." [39] It is difficult not to feel in the following passage—on coming home—the strength of Landor's recurrent need to be for a few moments, without disguise, a playwright or a novelist:

I returned and took possession of my cottage and free hold. The first door I opened was the barndoor. My arm-chair stood opposite me: I sat down on it, looking on the crimson bed until its colors were absorbed in my eyes, and the form itself had vanished. I did not meditate; I had no thoughts; sensation carried them away half-formed. I did not resist it, nor attempt to alter or direct it. I felt as if I were in the presence of those I loved, and as if any fresh motion of the mind or body would deprive me of it. [40]

Perhaps this dramatizing impulse is evidence not just of the storyteller in Landor, but rather of the whole poet. The case is clearer in my other example of the narrative kind of dialogue, the much shorter "Fra Filippo Lippi and Pope Eugenius the Fourth," which is a true conversation between two vigorous personalities. The portrait of the Pope emerges from it as he interrupts the leisurely narrative by Filippo about his being kidnapped by Barbary pirates and about his luxurious captivity under Abdul, who valued the pictures Filippo did for him. The Pope, with something of the power over Filippo that Abdul had had, is equally the captive of his genius and scapegrace charm. The reader is granted a still greater pleasure, in the beauty of the speech—mainly, and by right, what comes from the creative heart of Filippo. Since I shall quote a superb passage when we discuss Landor's style, at present it should be enough—thinking in terms of the dramatic—to call attention to the passage where the face of young Lucrezia hovers between Filippo and that of the Madonna he is painting, and the magnificent gesture with which "Resolving on a sudden that the object of my love should be the object of adoration to thousands, born and unborn, I swept my brush across the maternal face, and left a blank in heaven." [41]

One of the qualities shared by the last three quotations is a conclusiveness, a faculty for gathering up a situation and pressing out its juice; of telling what that is like and in such a way that there is no more to say; and then of letting the curtain fall. But the mind remains in its seat.

V *The Drama of Thought*

In a note to "The Emperor Alexander and Capo D'Istria," later reworked into the text of a revised version of "Florentine, English Visitor, and Landor," Landor admits that it is a blemish in a book to make any character reason more acutely or benevolently than he could have done in life; but he also asserts that it is a blemish the book would be the worse without: "The practice of Shakespeare and Sophocles is a better apology for me than I could offer of my own. If men were to be represented as they are, who would care about the greater part of the greatest? [42] . . . Principles and ideas are my objects: they must be reflected from high and low; but they must also be exhibited where people can see them best, and are most inclined to look at them." [43] There need be no difficulty over whether character or principles and ideas are more important to him. One does not exist without the other, and, for a man full of ideas, Landor was uncommonly interested in human beings.

It might be convenient to suggest that all the dialogues not yet mentioned belong to the drama of thought. To do so might, however, be foolish for two reasons. First, "dramatic" may be stretched to include everything in life, for everything may be thought of in terms of tensions, just as everything *must* be thought of in terms of comparison and contrast. Light and shade are dramatic, and there we are with the thesis at hand. But what we can say of everything in general cannot be said to clarify or define anything in particular. Second, in some of the dialogues the thought actually is dramatic, more so than anything else in them; and there is nothing comparable to this in the other dialogues.

There is a particular stress of thought, for instance, in "Galileo, Milton, and a Dominican." Galileo was no longer in prison when Milton actually visited Italy, but Landor needs to have it so. The Dominican who guards Galileo opens the door to Milton as if he were an angry visiting angel. For so long as the Dominican allows it (and the interview is short), the two men converse at ease about, among other things, the sort of welcome given to great minds—those who, "ages after their departure, are able to sustain the lowliest, and to exalt the highest" [44]—and about the toughness of truth. The contrast of the two men—one strong and hopeful, but only beginning his career, the other already a part of history—is moving enough; but neither that contrast nor the ideas as expressed can be given more than partial credit for the effect the dialogue has: it is the whole situation that, almost regardless of the individual thoughts that are spoken, loads the reader's mind with the fact of intelligence and truth in chains. We turn the last page in love with heresy.

"David Hume and John Home," like the rest of my examples of this kind of dialogue, depends almost entirely on the thoughts actually expressed. No one, however, can begin an argument in a vacuum; thoughts on most subjects already inhabit our minds; and, once the talk begins, we are drawn to a voice, a look, or the visage of character. This dialogue is a simple and friendly, though potentially explosive, confrontation of religion with morality, the two separate and independent. "Only give things their right direction," [45] says Hume, ". . . and there is room to move easily and pleasantly in the midst of them." Placidity and a reasoned regularity of habits will do what we need for ourselves. "Cousin" Home, however, sees life strictly in a religious frame: he is the lay missionary, a good man but easily set on fire. "Cousin" Hume is the civilized skeptic; there is a bottomless yawn in him, as well as an artillery that he declines to use. He it is who keeps the peace and who, while remaining himself and conceding nothing for mere politeness, gentles the waters and brings the bark of argument safe into harbor. To John Home, it's a poor Scotsman who has nothing better to say of holiness than that "all her ways are pleasantness, and all her paths are peace," [46] and to many a reader, no doubt, the sacred inscrutability of the question is evaded by Landor, and great problems are resolved by a pagan quietus.

Something of the same opposition of points of view goes on at much greater length in the dialogue "William Penn and Lord Peterborough." (It occurs to me that at least some of those experienced readers who fail to see any real thought in Landor are deprived of the capacity by previous conviction; if profundity is mystical, then Landor is not profound.) Peterborough is the famous commander, diplomat, and patron of letters. Because in religion and philosophy he is, to the degree permitted in his time, a free agent, he is even more impressively the civilized man of the world than Penn, who is the late seventeenth-century enthusiast tempered by sophistication, and a man of primitive and stern piety, with a genius for the just government of others. Penn is even a man among men, and he is something amiable beyond that, for he can reply to one of Peterborough's flights of gaiety, "God mend thee, madcap! Wilt thou come and live with us?" [47]

Peterborough has opinions to give the Quaker not only about service in armies but about the good the theater may do us: ". . . the amusement and merriment go to bed with man and wife, and something is left for the children the next morning at breakfast." [48] With liquid lucidity, Peterborough meanwhile reveals himself as a man who likes to feel his strength and his superiority to superior people. He likes to make his dent on life. The ambition of Penn, on the other hand, must be inferred by the black-hearted reader. Peterborough is a full-bodied and fully self-expressive gentleman, an infidel who argues pleasantly and humorously for the delights of culture—for dancing, singing, drawing, scientific curiosity, and the occasional privilege of irrational behavior.

That Peterborough often enough speaks for Landor, we know
from his other writings; Penn is sometimes allowed to quote from
his own. Though Penn could not be consistently a spokesman for
Landor, he is treated with complete respect, and is given some of
the strongest lines—for instance, his "Teach people to rule themselves, and they will neither bear violence nor inflict it." [49] To Penn,
Peterborough is a good young man, in spite of his conceiving of
energy in terms of acts of blood. The divergence of points of view
could hardly be more definite, but we could not wish for a more
civilized and richly profitable conversation. The elasticity of mind
is more evident in Peterborough, who can afford it: Penn is good;
Peterborough, delightful. "Are you not ashamed," says the infidel,
at the end of a fine speech by Penn on the power of holiness in this
unhopeful world—"Are you not ashamed of being so eloquent?" [50]

Altogether at intellectual odds are Diogenes and Plato in their
dialogue. We feel for a long time that Plato is at a disadvantage
from which only a different author could save him: he is expen-
sively and exquisitely dressed in the presence not only of philosophy,
which looks upon gewgaws without much favor, but of the super-
tramp among philosophers. The style of Diogenes is naked and
direct; and how is Plato, the magician of Greek prose, the weaver
of air-stuff, even to respond to him? He responds as a caricature
for the first forty pages; and only his unqualified admirers could
bleed much for him. He takes refuge in superciliousness, the defense
of the helplessly fastidious; and, from it, he falls back into effemi-
nate shock. "Aristoteles," says Diogenes (for one of Landor's
orthographical convictions is that we should be consistent: if not
"Themistocle," then not "Aristotle"),

Aristoteles, and all the rest of you, must have the wadding of straw
and saw-dust shaken out, and then we shall know pretty nearly your
real weight and magnitude.

Plato. A philosopher ought never to speak in such a manner of
philosophers.[51]

As for Plato's appearance, he dares say that "We may serve our
country, I hope, with clean faces." [52] He is even made capable, in
addition to pettiness, of a feeble malignancy, as when, in answer to
Diogenes' disapproval of the slaughter of the people of Melos, he
remarks, "I thought I heard Diogenes say he had no sympathy with
the mass of mankind: what could excite it so suddenly in behalf
of an enemy?" [53]

More pleasant is Landor's little characterizing joke, when Plato, having shown envy of Aristotle in his being made tutor of the son of Philip of Macedon, is given a petulant but resounding lapse of memory: "Knowing the arrogance of Philip, and the signs of ambition which his boy (I forget the name) hath exhibited so early. . . ." [54]

Diogenes could wish nothing better than what Landor has been doing to their victim. On the other hand, this dialogue is the legitimate expression of a difference in approaches to philosophy that has been of historical importance since at least the days of Aristotle. In Landor's terms, it is the concrete (Aristotle, Diogenes) against the abstract (Plato) and its progeny in ideas and behavior:

Diogenes. The bird of wisdom flies low, and seeks her food under hedges: the eagle himself would be starved if he always soared aloft and against the sun. The sweetest fruit grows near the ground, and the plants that bear it require ventilation and lopping. Were this not to be done in thy garden, every walk and alley, every plot and border, would be covered with runners and roots, with boughs and suckers. We want no poets or logicians or metaphysicians to govern us: we want practical men, honest men, continent men, unambitious men, fearful to solicit a trust, slow to accept, and resolute never to betray one. Experimentalists may be the best philosophers: they are always the worst politicians. Teach people their duties, and they will know their interests. Change as little as possible, and correct as much.[55]

The author's voice is recognizable enough in this excerpt. Readers will see in it a traditional distrust of ambition, a traditional respect for work and elementary social responsibility, and that devotion to our material world, as the source and end of our intellectual life, which poets and cobblers know and must know—and philosophers too, if they are to be of use to themselves and to us. The real philosopher, according to Landor's Diogenes, never "occupied his hours in tingeing and curling the tarnished plumes of prostitute Philosophy, or deemed anything worth his attention, care, or notice, that did not make men brave and independent." [56]

From what Landor says elsewhere, he was aware of the strength and acuteness of Plato's mind; and it is unnecessary to be horrified at his apparent inability to join the rest of us in our cultured preference for the immaterial.

It might be interesting to list, as evidence of the nature of

Landor's attack and its degree of thoroughness, the main topics of discussion as they come up in this dialogue:

1. What is a great man?
2. Virtues.
3. What is a true philosopher?
4. Modesty and merit.
5. Poverty and plenteousness of thought.
6. Hard-heartedness.
7. Moderation and sincerity.
8. Wisdom as opposed to philosophy.
9. The inequality of punishments.
10. Free will and necessity.
11. Sound *versus* meaning.
12. The curse of slavery.
13. Soldiers in a free state.
14. Religion *versus* philosophy.
15. Arguments over the soul.
16. Metaphysics and logic in dialogue.
17. The occult.
18. Aristotle compared with Plato.
19. Ideas of beauty.
20. History.
21. Intimacy with kings.
22. The falsehood in kingship.
23. Originality and variety in Plato.
24. Married philosophers.
25. That the characteristic does not define.
26. Fact in Plato.

By the time we reach the subject of history, there is real conversation; for the two men are thinking in company though fundamentally at odds. Though Diogenes has heretofore been wielding a whip, he is, throughout, more than an intellectual railer; he is almost attractively plain and sturdy, as well as the better Greek. Much has been made of the fact that, once in Italy, Landor, wanting to know what he thought of Plato, had polished his Greek and had spent a month or so reading the works in the original from end to end; he has been congratulated on being thus one of the few and castigated for occasional misreading. The modern reader may by this time be sure that Landor is no more ignorant than most of us, nor more obtuse.

On Socrates' being made by Plato to rank a beautiful vase below a beautiful horse, and that below a beautiful maiden, and that below the beauty of the immortal gods, Diogenes has a good deal to say. What is most pertinent to our own historically confused view of the subject is Landor's understanding that Plato was distorting the word "beauty" as it was used by all of Hellas—that the Greek concept of fitness and rightness left no room for comparisons between a horse and a vase.[57] And now, has Landor no sense of the value of metaphysics? Perhaps he has more than the average metaphysician:

Plato. I may venture then, in defence of my compositions, to argue that neither simple metaphysics nor strict logic would be endured long together in a dialogue.

Diogenes. Few people can endure them anywhere; but whatever is contradictory to either is intolerable. The business of a good writer is to make them pervade his works, without obstruction to his force or impediment to his facility; to divest them of their forms, and to mingle their potency in every particle.[58]

This is a thinker's confession that he is a man and that abstract thought does not take place up there but down here as an organic part of the life we know.

VI   *The Amalgam: Imaginary Conversation*

Thought and character together are the fundamental interest of most of the dialogues, and it is high time to admit that Landor chose well in naming them all *Imaginary Conversations*. Some space may profitably be devoted to commenting on a selection of dialogues that are of slight dramatic interest but are excellent examples of imaginary conversation between persons of historical or literary interest. It is perhaps not altogether odd that such conversations are between men, or between men and women, but not between women alone. (The letters in "Pericles and Aspasia" are another matter.) Prejudice, blindness, or wickedness in Landor caused him to refrain from confronting Hannah More with Aspasia, or Sappho with Lady Mary Wortley Montagu; but a glance at the section devoted, in the editorial tradition of Forster, to Dialogues of Famous Women indicates that to Landor women are, as thinkers, more interesting in the company of men (so the great blue-stockings and mistresses of salons seem to have felt) and that even then a little drama helps to make the wheels go round. It is, of course, possible that he could not imagine women discussing mere ideas for very long at a time; and perhaps he is not to be seriously blamed for this view. There is one dialogue of character and idea (of historical import) in which Princess Mary and Princess Elizabeth [59] arch their backs at each other, and I should call them very well observed —or imagined. The plumpness of Mary's understanding foretells no good for the England she is soon to rule; but the issues are men's issues—only accident threw them into the hands of successive queens; and those queens, while female, were not in all senses womanly.

"Both in the physical and the spiritual," said Sidney Colvin,[60] "Landor's feeling for the feminine is as strong as it is exquisite; there is no writer, Shakespeare alone once more excepted, who surpasses him in it." Havelock Ellis, in his introduction to the selection of imaginary conversations in the Camelot Classics, calls this judgment extravagant: "Tender and noble figures they often are, but even at the best seldom more than the personification of boundless resignation or self-sacrifice. He looks at them generally from the outside and as a painter, not dramatically from the inside. He describes them as objects of love, but they possess scarcely the most elementary capacity of response to love." [61]

But Lady Blessington, who was neither the personification of boundless resignation nor that of the New Woman, declared to Landor: "No man ever could define the feelings and thoughts of woman, that is, the most pure and unsophisticated portion of the sex, as you can. You enter even beyond the veil of that temple (in woman's heart) so seldom penetrated, and her *naïveté* and tenderness acquire new charms by your translation of them." [62] The truth about the sexes is what they regret in themselves and what they wish were so.

For me, as for Colvin also, a little of the surface girlishness and its fluttering eyelids is too much. Though Landor was, from sympathy and plain fondness, better acquainted with attractive young girls than most men of mature years have ever been, his success as an artist is mostly with adult women. The breakdown of the dying Ternissa, in the first conversation of "Menander and Epicurus," is fine. Not a bust of her but her full-length statue is what we want, says the middle-aged Epicurus, whom she loves; and Ternissa opens her eyes wide, turns away, and buries her face in the pillow, saying, "almost inaudibly, 'O mother, mother!' " [63]

There is no such reality, pathetic or otherwise, in the girls in Landor's favorite "Epicurus, Leontion, and Ternissa," the mawkishness of which almost overwhelms the ideas of Epicurus, whose tranquil beauty it threatens to turn into a confection. Landor has given the Garden a hothouse air in which the intellect would droop were it not for words of strength and freshness from Epicurus, which rise above us as they are spoken and gather in sculptured clouds along the horizon of the dialogue.

The Epicurus of Landor—the Epicurus that inhabited Landor himself—is independent yet not egocentric; in other words, in the elimination of the causes of pain, he cares as much for truth as is consistent with being human:

All schools of philosophy, and almost all authors, are rather to be frequented for exercise than for freight; but this exercise ought to acquire us health and strength, spirits and good-humor. There is none of them that does not supply some truth useful to every man, and some untruth equally so to the few that are able to wrestle with it. If there were no falsehood in the world, there would be no doubt; if there were no doubt, there would be no inquiry; if no inquiry, no wisdom, no knowledge, no genius: and Fancy herself would lie muffled up in her robe, inactive, pale, and bloated. I wish we could demonstrate the existence of utility in some other evils as easily as in this.[64]

The world is not overrun with such lovers of thinking, of clear-headedness, of clean language, of the air they live in.

Speaking of Theophrastus, Leontion says:

In order to display his elegance of language, he runs wherever he can lay a censure on you, whether he believes in its equity or not.

Epicurus. This is the case with all eloquent men, and all disputants. Truth neither warms nor elevates them, neither obtains for them profit nor applause.

Ternissa. I have heard wise remarks very often and very warmly praised.

Epicurus. Not for the truth in them, but for the grace, or because they touched the spring of some preconception or some passion. Man is a hater of truth, a lover of fiction.[65]

The sententious ease about these observations may hide from inexperienced minds the fact that they come from close and candid scrutiny. Great generalizations decorate the walls of the memory for years, for decades, before a bit of experience, of firsthand observation, may make one of them for the first time jump alive out of its frame. Even when truth is not hard to bear, what would one do with it—and how would one do without the bevy of substitutes, some of them handmaidens to truth itself, that caress and soothe, that entice, that prepare the couch?

Philosophy, says Epicurus, requires solitude: "To be wise indeed, and happy and self-possessed, we must often be alone." [66] In company, communication is the object, and the "prime excellence" [67] in writing is perspicuity. The pleasures of walking together in the country, of refreshing the skin, the muscles, the lungs, the nose

itself, help those who disagree on "speculative points" to know
one another better in what is undeniable, for in such ways hearts
are brought together.[68] The retired philosopher has more than this
to say of life in society; for instance (and this is Landor's idea),
that temperance is of most merit as a virtue when it is "the support
of civility and politeness," [69] which themselves are the support of
peace and harmony. Temperance alone was not enough—though
temperance in perfection would, says Landor's Epicurus, be perfect
justice; a special object was needed for what temperance we are
capable of, and it was supplied. Politeness is not love, but it is more
easily called up and put to work.

This dialogue is Landor writing under difficulties: how to deal
with the warmest sentiments of tender affection between two young
girls and a middle-aged philosopher; and how to write like one of
the remembered minds of the ages.

The other conversations chosen for brief comment might be
divided into three groups—limited but loosely controlled, limited
and tightly controlled, unlimited and relaxed. They are not chosen
with any regard to their dates, but it happens that in terms of first
publication of individual conversations (we know little about their
genesis) each group spreads from the 1820's, when Landor was
entering upon or well into his fifties, to 1846 or 1853, when he
was at the beginning or end of his seventies. It is all mature work,
with no signs of growth, shift, or decline of powers. The same may
be said of the conversations already commented upon, of which the
least impressive, "Rhadamistus and Zenobia," appeared in Ablett's
Literary Hours in 1837, at what some might call the height of
Landor's career.

The height of a career that had no height and was no career
is determined by standing him on two large works, *Pericles and
Aspasia* (1836) and the "Pentameron" (1837); they are first rate,
but so are many of his shorter ones, before and after. Again, the
feeble "Beniowski and Aphanasia" came out in 1828; in 1828
appeared also the masterly "Bossuet and the Duchess of Fontanges"; and in 1829 the great discursive dialogues "William Penn
and Lord Peterborough" and "Diogenes and Plato." All that can
be learned from these comparative dates is that Landor's intelligence sometimes failed when his emotion was involved; the same
may be said of any well-constituted person.

a. LIMITED BUT LOOSELY CONTROLLED. Landor's two long

conversations between Samuel Johnson and John Horne (Tooke), the political reformer and author of the philological work *The Diversions of Purley,* are almost unreadable except by an etymologist and student of orthography with an interest in the dimmer and more eccentric byways. A number of pages at a stretch are interesting and amusing to anyone who cares about language, but a hundred pages of guesswork on the principles of linguistic change, of personal conclusions arrived at by haphazard parallels and analogies, of unhistorical and inconsistent purism are altogether too much.

The cussedness of the two strong individualists in itself is full of flavor—Landor's, really. To generalize baldly, Landor would follow the great old writers in the apparent principles of their usage; and, like them, he would spell more as we speak. Here, it seems, he was willing to overlook personal and regional peculiarities and to depend on custom for a questionable consensus; for he said but did not write "goolden" and "woonderful" and "laylock" and "obleege"—and, according to some, he dropped his "aitches" (though he tells us in "Archdeacon Hare and Walter Landor" that nobody says "an heavy load," "an heavenly joy," "an holy man," "an hermit," "an high place," "an huge monster," "an holly-bough," "an happy day"). As appears from notes in his own copy of *Last Fruit Off an Old Tree,*[70] Landor was in his last decade still haplessly correcting the spelling of his publishers, taking the "u" out of "honour" and "labouring," "splendour" and "colourist"; changing "although" to "altho," "still" to "stil"; an unaccented "there" to "ther"; and adding a sturdy old "k" to "catholic."

The limitation of these dialogues is in their subject, not in their human interest, which after all is what their science itself amounts to. The discussion is lively and conversational, and it is carried on by notable personalities. Landor's Johnson is brief of expression but luxuriant of wit; he has always something in reserve: "It is better and pleasanter to talk generally on great and high subjects than minutely. Who would examine that could expatiate?" [71] When asked by Tooke if in his travels he had ever happened to see gossamer, Johnson replies that he had seen it five miles from Lichfield but that "latterly my travels were in Scotland, where there was no plant to support it." [72] Of the many attempts after Boswell to "do a Doctor Johnson," Landor's is certainly as good as any. There is no strain in it and no appeal to a panting audience; it is all intellect.

Landor's Tooke is triumphant pedantry mixed with sense; he is honored by his creator with aphorism. In answer to the question "what language do you like?" he says: "The best in all countries is that which is spoken by intelligent women, of too high rank for petty affectation, and of too much request in society for deep study." [73] To suggest that Landor himself could not believe any such thing is to belie his knowledge of life and letters.

Another special subject is that of "Milton and Andrew Marvel." In it, character is in abeyance; the discussion, though far from intense, is enough to occupy the mind of writer and reader; it is a common-sense discussion of possible principles of comedy. The only surprise in it is an attack on Aristophanes for failing to discriminate in his ridicule. Common sense is in charge, even on the tide of Miltonic disapproval: "I hold it abominable to turn into derision what is excellent. To render undesirable what ought to be desired is the most mischievous and diabolical of malice." [74]

Marvel (as Landor spells it) appears again in a conversation in which he tries to convince Bishop Parker of the worth of Milton. Marvel speaks sardonically as well as with hot indignation of those who could be cold or supercilious toward so elevated and generous a mind. Parker, who, according to the private chronology of this dialogue, has newly insinuated himself (hard work, sometimes, insinuation) into his bishopric, tries to dodge Marvel's criticisms of place-seekers and place-awarders by at one point declaring, "Really, Mr. Marvel, I do not understand metaphors." [75] This revelation augurs well for the whole discussion.

The most interesting passages in the Marvel-Parker dialogue are not those that develop a particular aspect of seventeenth-century politics and church history, but general remarks, such as that "Municipalities—in other words, small republics—are a nation's mainstay against aristocratical and regal encroachments"; [76] or that "Prudent and quiet people will choose their churches as they choose their ale-houses,—partly for the wholesomeness of the draught, and partly for the moderation of the charges"; [77] or that "As the pearl ripens in the obscurity of its shell, so ripens in the tomb all the fame that is truly precious." [78] There is, however, a heaving of consciousness of character in the piece when Parker late in the day, but rapidly, turns from a defensive coldness to a polite inclination to listen. This change follows immediately upon his failure to catch a subtlety of Marvel's (he thought Marvel was paying him the great compliment of not questioning his morals), and nothing about it is obvious or even a touch overdone.

"Archdeacon Hare and Walter Landor," the latest (1853) of these dialogues to appear, belongs in the "limited" group because it begins as another crowded discussion of the spellings and uses of words; having scared off most readers, Hare and Landor stray into literature. It is good talk about *Gebir,* Southey, Wordsworth, Juvenal, Lucan, Statius, and the crime of vaticide. "Fancy," says Walter Landor of yet another literary subject, "is Imagination in her youth and adolescence": "Fancy is always excursive; Imagination, not seldom, is sedate. . . . Vigorous thought, elevated sentiment, just expression, development of character, power to bring man out from the secret haunts of his soul, and to place him in strong outline against the sky, belong to Imagination." [79]

So the tea party goes on, in which we distinguish between two words where one will do, dreaming that one limitless but recognizable phenomenon comes in two pieces because it is pleasant to think in terms of duality. It is often Landor's work to dispose of such nonsense; here he did away with Fancy in his first sentence and brought her back to life in his next, because she was such a charming habit. It is good talk, though, and the speakers know it:

Archdeacon Hare. Are you aware how much thought you have here been throwing away?
Walter Landor. My dear friend! thought is never thrown away: wherever it falls, or runs, or rests, it fertilizes.[80]

We could say as much for the prose works of Landor; and it is in this conversation that we find what must not go unquoted: "I have published five volumes of *Imaginary Conversations:* cut the worst of them through the middle, and there will remain in this decimal fraction quite enough to satisfy my appetite for fame. I shall dine late; but the dining-room will be well lighted, the guests few and select." [81] Critics and academics, in their obscure and ominous need to go in crowds, have seen to it that that last sentence is better known than all the rest of his prose.

b. LIMITED AND TIGHTLY CONTROLLED. In turning to what stricter control of a limited subject can do for imaginary conversation, I do not intend to underrate the pleasures of the foregoing. The limitation of nineteenth-century political history, however, has lowered the value of most of Landor's political dialogues,

controlled or uncontrolled, because of too much topical thinking
and topical reference. Landor had to have his say on involved
affairs that are forever removed from us as an instant cause of
feeling; that does not mean that a reader who enjoys Landor will
not see what he can get (and there is always something to be got)
from all of them. At least one of these dialogues is completely
successful because, though severely limited in its origin, it speaks of
things that are familiar to all of us, because it is not allowed to
wander, and because in its economy and concentration it emerges
from turmoil as a comedy.

The dialogue referred to is "Mr. Pitt and Mr. Canning" (both
names which could for many years be counted upon to send the
blood into Landor's head). It begins in a promising way:

Pitt. Dear Canning, my constitution is falling to pieces, as fast as,
your old friend Sheridan would tell you, the constitution of the country is, under my management. Of all men living, you are the person
I am most desirous to appoint my successor. My ambition is unsatis-
fied while any doubt of my ability to accomplish it remains upon
my mind. Nature has withholden from me the faculty of propagating
my species: nor do I at all repine at it, as many do; since every
great man must have some imbecile one very near him, if not next to
him, in descent.

Canning. I am much flattered, sir, by your choice of me, there
being so many among your relatives who might expect it for themselves. However this is only another instance of your great disinterest-
edness.

Pitt. You may consider it in that light if you will; but you must
remember that those who have exercised power long together, and
without control, seldom care much about affinities.[82]

The handling is sure, with the characters' unconscious self-reve-
lation and self-mockery balanced between the two, restrained and
dignified, as in the perfect dance of satire the bodies are conscious
and the minds only half aware: "Excuse me," they say, if they touch
each other, while in blank solitude they commune with their own
mirrors in heaven. Comedy is satire in love with its victim; and in
this conversation the spirit of comedy has spread its wings over
the noisy and awkward nestlings of controversy.

Here are the possibilities of a deathbed frankness. "For a
successful minister," says Pitt, "three things are requisite on
occasion"—and "on occasion" calls up the infinite languor of
power: "to speak like an honest man, to act like a dishonest one,

and to be indifferent which you are called." (The responsibilities
are heavy, but see the grace of our broad shoulders in the capable
slow rhythms of our prose.) "Talk of God," Pitt continues, "as
gravely as if you believed in him. Unless you do this, I will not say,
what our Church does, you will be damned; but, what indeed is a
politician's true damnation, you will be dismissed. Most very good
men are stout partisans of some religion, and nearly all very bad
ones. . . ." [83] Canning wishes to be modest as well as confident,
but his reply, in the glibness of its cynicism, shows him to be not
so much his own man as a product of the university.

> *Pitt.* . . . You are brilliant by the multitude of flaws, and not by the
> clearness nor the quantity of light.
> *Canning.* On second thoughts, I am not quite sure, not perfectly
> satisfied, that it is, as one may say, altogether mine. [84]

So, in addition to the illustrations of public life as we know it, we
are regaled with epigram and with the music of prose that is willed
and conducted through every phrase.

"Lucian and Timotheus," whose special subject is Lucian's opinion of Christianity, is at least as well ordered as any dialogue
by Lucian. It is also more concentrated on its subject and (though
only a Classicist, presumably, is qualified to judge) is a stronger
piece of imaginative prose. Lucian begins well by answering the
eternal complaint of the tyrannous and the timid against "destruc-
tive criticism." He is so bold as to suggest that an error should be
removed as soon as it is detected, "although it may be out of our
competence to state and establish what is right"; lies, he says—all
evils—should be eradicated like weeds, "if only because the
temporary absence of evil is an advantage." [85]

Lucian now turns to the religion of Timotheus, with the reminder that the true and holy is proof against ridicule—a metaphysical argument stolen from Timotheus' side for the purposes,
as Timotheus rightly complains, of an atheist. As for atheists,
there are almost as few of them in the world as Christians, says
Lucian, indulging, for Landor's sake, in a hoary self-protective
quibble that continues to be most popular. But none of this prefatory material suggests the easy discourse of the old pagan, his
inventiveness, and the quiet pleasure he has in communing with
himself while directing his words at pitiful Cousin Timotheus.
Lucian's talk is that of a moralist and wit who has seen or heard

of everything; his style has the flow of conversation and the unhurried and unnoticeable calculation of mastery.

It is the antihuman that Lucian dislikes, as well as what is unctuously called "the spiritual." Timotheus says there is something so spiritual about Plato that many Christians believe him to have been "partially enlightened from above"—to which Lucian replies that he hopes we all are.[86] When Timotheus congratulates himself on living under Grace, Lucian remarks: "I also live under Grace, O Timotheus! and I venerate her for the pleasures I have received at her hands. I do not believe she has quite deserted me." [87] Philosophy is for the benefit of the race, he says. Such practicality is an effect of imagination, as is the sympathy that preceded it. Its natural charm almost tempts Timotheus to set in order his ideas of greatness and thus his definitions of good and evil. What do we teach our children about morals? The pedagogues, says Lucian,

would punish a thirsty child for purloining a bunch of grapes from a vineyard, and the same men on the same day would insist on his reverence for the subverter of Tyre, the plunderer of Babylon, and the incendiary of Persepolis. And are these men teachers? are these men philosophers? are these men priests? Of all the curses that ever afflicted the earth, I think Alexander was the worst. Never was he in so little mischief as when he was murdering his friends.[88]

Yet he built this noble city, says Everyman Timotheus; Lucian replies with a reminder about an architect and some stonecutters and plasterers and with a disrespectful reference to the glorious spoilers of civilized hopes. Lucian and Landor claim some approbation for having taxed us with the fraudulence and the inhumanity of what we admire.

c. UNLIMITED AND RELAXED. At the end of "Rousseau and Malesherbes," the excellent Malesherbes has tossed in the direction of Rousseau several rhetorical questions. "I could answer you," says Rousseau:

but my mind has certain moments of repose, or rather of oscillation, which I would not for the world disturb. Music, eloquence, friendship, bring and prolong them.

Malesherbes. Enjoy them, my dear friend, and convert them if possible to months and years. It is as much at your arbitration on what theme you shall meditate, as in what meadow you shall botanize; and you have as much at your option the choice of your thoughts, as of the keys in your harpsichord.

Rousseau. If this were true, who could be unhappy?

Malesherbes. Those of whom it is not true. Those who from want of practice cannot manage their thoughts, who have few to select from, and who, because of their sloth or of their weakness, do not roll away the heaviest from before them.[89]

Surely these words were most true of Landor. They bring with them a strong sense of the happiness that went into the making of the *Imaginary Conversations,* and that is as much a component of their perfume as of their curiosity and their love of language. Such art as Landor's floods the mind; the exercise of it must have excluded the disharmony of an ordinary day.

To give rein to mood and fancy—as Landor does in conversations of the sort that are unlimited in subject and relaxed, as conversation may sometimes be, and still be good—is to present the reader with the best elements of the familiar essay, relieved and enriched with elements of drama and with unlooked-for points of view. In a "Chaucer, Boccaccio, and Petrarca," at times, character, situation, conversation itself are swept together into lyric. For example, in other dialogues Italy is made to feel the whip, for Landor had had unpleasant dealings there with landowners and bureaucrats. In this dialogue, however, he puts into Chaucer's mouth some other kinds of experience that Chaucer may have had as well as he:

Chaucer. Yet, Messer Giovanni, I never journeyed so far through so enchanting a scenery as there is almost the whole of the way from Arezzo to Rome, particularly round Terni and Narni and Perugia.

Our master, Virgil, speaks of dreams that swarm upon the branches of one solitary elm. In this country, more than dreams swarm upon every spray and leaf; and every murmur of wood or water comes from and brings with it inspiration. Never shall I forget the hour when my whole soul was carried away from me by the cataract of Terni, and when all things existing were lost to me in its stupendous waters. The majestic woods that bowed their heads before it; the sun that was veiling his glory in mild translucent clouds over the furthest course of the river; the moon, that suspended her orb in the very centre of it—seemed ministering Powers, themselves in undiminished admiration of the marvel they had been looking on through un-numbered ages.[90]

Majesty and the marvel of dreams that swarm upon a leaf choose the language that must express them. There is nothing merely conventional about the grand acquiescence of the woods, the generous restraint of the sun, the tremendous delicacy of the moon in her far fingerings of her own position, and the depths of distance transmitted to us in the fading of that cadence "over the furthest course of the river."

The expansive form that Landor works in can be called "form" only because a certain gathering of mind and senses is named Landor, and its expression when the man is most aware cannot be formless. The variety of experience that clamors for expression would in most other writers be an irritant. In Landor, that variety is harmonized by style, which is an evidence of self-mastery—not of the self that the world sees in the street but of the one the writer knows alone, for only he has been in lifelong quest of it.

Having lived in the mind of Epicurus, we are invited to pause in that of Cicero, as he and his brother Quinctus talk at ease of immortality, of government equitable and unjust, of history and biography, and of the psychological value of horticulture. One of the most satisfying of many such excursions is a secret visit of Caesar to Lucullus, in his Apennine villa, to ask help against Pompey. Lucullus refuses; but meanwhile talk has flourished between them, of the alternation in history of irreligion with fanaticism, one perpetually leading to the other; of historians (to converse of such men as Thucydides is held to be conducive not only to virtue but to health); [91] of a verbal inelegancy or two in Cicero, along with genius and power; of the equinoxes in human life; of strawberries and milk, which Lucullus prefers to his imported melons, now cooling in the snow. A reader may expand in such surroundings.

More intimate, though profoundly urbane, is "La Fontaine and De La Rochefoucault," of which Crump says in his note, "The Conversation is one of the best. Both the characters are well kept up, and there is very little Theology." The main idea is to oppose to La Rochefoucauld's belief that men are ruled by self-interest the thought of another fine writer that it is not so much selfishness in the form of egoism as love of power, of possession. At least that is how La Fontaine sees it when he can for a moment transfer his attention from dogs and cats to men. Under the gentle candor of La Fontaine, to whom it seems that "what is natural is not depraved,— that depravity is deflection from nature" [92]; to whom nothing is holy that seems to lessen the beneficence of God, and who warns us that to ascribe ungentleness to God is to give a deadly license to men—under the softness of these words is not a man of steel, but something equally formidable—a man coldly indifferent to everything that is not spontaneously warm. Thus, given Landor's wit, the fencing match is a good one. But a reader is gratefully conscious, all along, of small matters closely observed—for instance, a proof of modesty in dogs: "Look at a dog's eyes; and he half-closes them, or gently turns them away, with a motion of the lips, which he licks languidly, and of the tail, which he stirs tremulously, begging your forbearance." [93] Speaking of La Fontaine's dog, which has taken possession of his chair, La Rochefoucauld asks, "Of what breed is he? for I know nothing of dogs"; and La Fontaine exclaims: "And write so well!" [94]

Or we may breakfast with Montaigne, whose beautiful common sense, in "Joseph Scaliger and Montaigne," can reduce the highfalutin to the level of fundamental things faster and with less violence than any acid. This wholly delightful little conversation covers a large part of life in its mention of a few household matters —of which life itself is the main. Pride in learning, in righteousness, in knowledge of the world, in maturity of intellect, and in family are all casually and amiably knocked on the head as Montaigne, by a word and a wave of the hand, demonstrates the value of domesticity, of food and drink over abstract ideas, of people over personages, of playful naturalness over stiff self-consciousness, of goodness over correctness—in fact, a whole set of values, as our somber, self-bemused society would call them. One extract will have to suffice; in tone and thought, it may represent the dialogue as a whole.

Scaliger. This, I perceive, is the antechamber to your library: here are your every-day books.

Montaigne. Faith! I have no other. These are plenty, methinks; is not that your opinion?

Scaliger. You have great resources within yourself and therefore can do with fewer.

Montaigne. Why, how many now do you think here may be?

Scaliger. I did not believe at first that there could be above fourscore.

Montaigne. Well! are fourscore few?—are we talking of peas and beans?

Scaliger. I and my father (put together) have written well nigh as many.

Montaigne. Ah! to write them is quite another thing: but one reads books without a spur, or even a pat from our Lady Vanity. How do you like my wine?—it comes from the little knoll yonder: you cannot see the vines, those chestnut-trees are between.[95]

There in natural speech is the sound of the eternal simplicities, as we hear it from Aesop to Erasmus. Shall we inscribe it on the walls of a modern university? And if one does not read books without a spur, is one capable of discussing those who do? Does one, incidentally, know in the depths of the bowels that "How do you like my wine?" was not a change of subject? Even the little knoll is something loved, and the chestnut trees bear nourishment and delectation.

c. (1) *Humanity: Italian.* Landor wrote no fuller human document than the *Pentameron,* which is the imaginary record of conversation during a five days' visit of Petrarch to the ailing Boccaccio in his villa outside the walls of Certaldo. The *Pentameron* is slightly encumbered with an introduction and epilogue by the imaginary finder of the manuscript and by some words of its imaginary translator. It is brought into touch with common life by Boccaccio's maid Assunta, a sprightly young woman who I believe is blameless, but who is otherwise altogether worthy of Boccaccio's world—and of ours, if we could hear a little of the poetry of earth. One of the best things in Landor is her story of the reluctant Maria, as Maria and Luca enter the porch of the church to be married: " 'Luca! It is not yet too late to leave me.' He would have kissed her, but her face was upon his shoulder."

And when Assunta has finished her tale (the reader must watch her eyes):

Having now performed her mission and concluded her narrative, she bowed, and said,

"Excuse me, Riverenza! excuse me, Signor Padrone! my arm aches with this great fish."

Then, bowing again, and moving her eyes modestly toward each, she added, "with permission!" and left the chamber.[96]

Otherwise the dialogue belongs to Boccaccio and Petrarch (whom Landor insists on calling Petrarca). They talk long of Dante, but their real subject is poetry and life. We are left in no doubt of Landor's revulsion at Dante's limitations, not as a constructor and composer, but as a human being. Boccaccio is once able to remark almost tranquilly of the rapt builder of hell, that "His flames are too fierce for you and me: we had trouble enough with milder." [97] Boccaccio feels more strongly than that; he groans with all the weight of his blessed mortality: "Sometimes I have been ready to believe, as far as our holy faith will allow me, that it were better our Lord were nowhere, than torturing in his inscrutable wisdom, to all eternity, so many myriads of us poor devils, the creatures of his hands. Do not cross thyself so thickly, Francesco!" [98]

How comes it, Boccaccio asks, that Dante, only one of us poor devils, should have been so tirelessly vindictive and vituperative, should have taken such long and infinitesimally laborious a pleasure in devising a world of endless torment? Lucretius the atheist had more dignity and loving-kindness in him. To Landor's Boccaccio, as to Landor himself, a fascination with darkness and cruelty is intolerable. If the young poets wish to be healthy and vigorous, says Boccaccio, "let them open their bosoms to the breezes of Sunium; for the air of Latium is heavy and overcharged." [99] He is prescribing for the diseases of Romanticism, this old humanist: "What is there lovely in poetry unless there be moderation and composure?" [100]

In the middle of a discussion of style, Petrarch offers some advice which is less necessary to Boccaccio than to the reader: "Enter into the mind and heart of your own creatures: think of them long, entirely, solely: never of style, never of self, never of critics, cracked or sound." [101] As characters, Petrarch and Boccaccio are not strongly distinguished from each other, speech by speech. Boccaccio, however, is more vitally tied to the earth, less able to sound detached than the other, yet no less wise. Boccaccio is here and now; Petrarch is perspective. Petrarch is often right, but Boccaccio, less exquisite, is our center. Petrarch is our friend; Boccaccio, ourselves.

Boccaccio's is as close to the Shakespearean mind (without the language) as, with no effort to transform himself, Landor can get. He is a little of everybody worth being. Speaking of a chest of letters, he says, "Leave me the memory of all my friends, even of the ungrateful." [102] And what a cat he has! The wondrous creature has a tail like a royal scepter, like the wand of a magician. "In cleanliness he is a very nun." [103] The conversation is not only full of thought; it is full of affection and sunlight and hints of flowers.

c. (2) *Humanity: Hellenic.* "Hate with me," writes Aspasia to

Cleone, "if you can hate anything, . . . the vengeance that rises above piety, above sorrow; the vengeance that gloats upon its prostrate victim." [104] She is referring to the state of mind of Electra (for it was to Aspasia's pen that Landor gave his "Shades of Agamemnon and of Iphigeneia" and his "Death of Clytemnestra"). Landor was more Classical in spirit than Euripides.

Pericles and Aspasia, not a dialogue at all, but a book of letters, is Landor's longest and most ambitious tribute to the Hellenic achievement. Unlike the *Pentameron,* it has a colorless purity about it, a whiteness that may be a reflection of what to later ages has been left of the once gaudy sculpture and architecture of Greece. This book cannot be taken for history; it need only be accepted for what it is—as beautiful an illustration of the blander aspects of wisdom as there can well be in any language.

The work is held together by a thread of story, from the introduction of Aspasia into the life of Pericles; through the heresy trial of Anaxagoras (and of Aspasia), set going by politics; through the pestilence, which causes Aspasia to establish herself with little Pericles in Thessaly; and to the death of Pericles the Great. In the course of the book, Landor presents a miscellany of his own most Attic and Ionian thoughts through the letters of Aspasia (whom, as a learned, brilliant, and beautiful courtesan—the latter is not stressed—he trusts to express them well) and of her several correspondents. Except where general ideas are concerned, Aspasia is recognizably a woman; her friend Cleone is clearly one; Pericles is a great man rendered almost human by main force of resolution on the part of Landor. The best characters are Alcibiades and Anaxagoras: Alcibiades, beautiful, avid of kisses, brave, wayward, and wild, is a triumphant adaptation of the material given Landor by Plato and Plutarch; Anaxagoras, every wise man's philosopher, is a friend even Aspasia was lucky to have.

We meet Thucydides, Sophocles, and Euripides; and we hear comments on many of the great events of the time. For perspective and relief, we are given numerous verses as well as general observations. "I do believe, Aspasia," says Cleone, "that studious men, who look so quiet, are the most restless men in existence." [105] Add to this conclusion, which at this very moment a statistical study of universities would seem to be trying unnecessarily to establish, a generalization on the vulgar: "The vulgar have not *their* prejudices: they have the prejudices of those who ought to remove them if they had any." [106] We are reminded in other terms of the effects of superiority on any society; for instance, that "We are all insurgents against the despotism of excellence." [107]

For those of us to whom it is open, there is a refuge from most ills (this is Anaxagoras to Aspasia): "You, Pericles, and myself, have a world of our own, into which no Athenian can enter without our permission. Study, philosophize, write poetry. These things I know are difficult when there is a noise in the brain; but begin, and the noise ceases. The mind, slow in its ascent at first, accelerates every moment, and is soon above the hearing of frogs and the sight of brambles." [108]

Yet for everyone there are notes on realities easier of access, whose accessibility offers the pleasures of the intimate: "the stiff reverted little horns" of cyclamen, with evidence of a nose in courteous propinquity; [109] the smell, nostalgic for some, of peeled willow; [110] and more generally, but deeply, such a cry of mortal observation as Cleone's, that "The very beautiful rarely love at all." [111]

Before the end of the letters, Aspasia is convinced that there is no god but Eros—not the little boy nuisance of Anacreon but the old god, the ineluctable: "the framer, the preserver of the world, the pure Intelligence! All wisdom that is not enlightened and guided by him is perturbed and perverted." [112]

In Landor's *Pentameron* the poetry of the man Boccaccio was to show as much. I think it showed more. The gates into harmony are plain as Doric, but they are not white except with heat; and there is a roar of bulls and dragons in the way.

CHAPTER 5

Prose: Criticism

NO ONE can read a page of Landor without being conscious that he is in the presence of a critical mind, and the reader of this present book has been deluged with Landor's opinions, all easily enough distinguished, whether spoken in play or dialogue, from those of which he disapproved or which he could not possibly have held. It might be useful, however, to bring together some of the results of Landor's lifelong weighing and passing of judgment, with the hope that a little contrived order and coherence will not misrepresent him.

I *Politics*

Politics and religion are almost as fundamental to the work of Landor as they are to civilized life—naturally enough, considering their importance to conversation in circles or societies where conversation exists at all. That he has much to say about politics is due to his strong sense of self and to the embattled individualism of one who was very nearly a man of action. But he could never have been anything but his own man, and his independence and perfectionism gave him to contemplation and to us. His Horace, in speaking of his early days in Athens, says that there he was "wild for freedom, as the most generous and intelligent boys are apt to be." [1] Landor was wild for it all his life and was able to afford it.

In his mid-twenties, Landor's mentor, Samuel Parr, tried to start him off as a political journalist. Landor had already published *To the Burgesses of Warwick* (1797), a pamphlet against a new tax bill and the Tories of his neighborhood; but elaborating on the ideas of Parr, or even working with a party, was impossible for him. [2] In the politics of his earlier life, Landor was for Fox, and against Pitt, Canning, and all others who could not bring themselves to work for Reform. He never forgave France for abandoning its revolution. His love of liberty, however, caused him to support republics and not democracies and to denounce a mob or a man for the assumption of power.

Like writers of the earlier age—like Swift, Fielding, and many others—Landor detested what history calls "the great man." He did so not out of envy or pettiness, for no ancient Roman thrilled more to the depths than he did to great courage, magnanimity, loyalty, justice—qualities of noble men. He detested (what his clean, clear mind and broad sympathies revolted at) the cheap paradox of history and every present day that is forced upon a not-willing mankind: that exceeding strength, persistence, and insensibility are greatness. In an address to Pope Pius IX, part of the preface to his *Hellenics,* Landor says that God's two greatest curses are "uncontrolled power and perverted intellect" [3]—Buonaparte's, and our, affliction. In another mood, at another gate of the subject, Landor may have Pericles say, "with one of his grave smiles," ". . . being a politician, I know that a single false step is a fall, and a fall is ruin. We may begin wrong, and continue so with impunity; but we must not deviate from wrong to right." [4]

Or, in a letter on Lord Brougham, he may stab with a definition: "I may be asked if I think myself capable of setting right so great a personage. No, indeed. Great personages are never to be set right. This is the only criterion I know of greatness." [5] Anger overflows the cup at times:

A housebreaker is condemned to die: a citybreaker is celebrated by an inscription over the gate. The murder of thousands, soon perpetrated and past, is not the greatest mischief he does: it is followed by the baseness of millions, deepening for ages. Every virtuous man in the universe is a member of that grand Amphictyonic council, which should pass sentence on the too powerful, and provide that it be duly executed. It is just and it is necessary that those who pertinaciously insist on an unnatural state of society should suffer by the shock things make in recovering their equipoise.[6]

In "Demosthenes and Eubulides," in "Landor, English Visitor, and Florentine," and elsewhere, on the basis that one brave man might save a nation from misery, Landor speaks for tyrannicide: "It is sanctioned by the laws of Solon, and sustained by the authority of Cicero and Aristoteles." [7]

Landor abhors the monolith. We are told by his Franklin that monarchy is close to anarchy, in that "no number is so near to nothing as one," [8] and that self-rule has been surrendered for rule by an ill-informed person who is likely to be capricious as well as intractable. Not all monarchs need be of this description, but one would be enough to prove the point. Diogenes, addressing Plato, is anarchism speaking either for itself or for a humane republic so wise as never to be great:

There is nothing so absurd that the ignorant have not believed: they have believed, and will believe for ever, what thou wouldst teach; namely, that others who never saw them, never are likely to see them, will care more about them than they should care about themselves. This pernicious fraud begins with perverting the intellect, and proceeds with seducing and corrupting the affections, which it transfers from the nearest to the most remote, from the dearest to the most indifferent. It enthralls the freedom both of mind and body; it annihilates not only political and moral but, what nothing else however monstrous can do, even arithmetical proportions, making a unit more than a million.[9]

In the conversation of Machiavelli and Michel-Angelo, Machiavelli criticizes democracy as cheapening all things and, according to the ancient formula, as leading to despotism. Michel-Angelo says, on the other hand, that all governments fall into despotism and that there is nothing to do to prevent it; but, in the course of things, Providence will liberate them, after which the usual changes will repeat themselves. Landor's view of men and their governments is a somber one, the kind that always used to be held by men who in an old-fashioned and unforced way read history as moderns read novels. What other view could there be? The great historians themselves dropped their heads on their breasts at the unending record of misery, stupidity, and scoundrelism.

Landor's Demosthenes, who should be listened to, tells us that every man would be a republican "if he did not expect to carry off sooner or later, from under another system, what never could belong to him rightfully, and what cannot (he thinks) accrue to him from this." [10] (The use of the word "republican" must remind an American that the wheel of political change is still turning.) Landor maintains his hold on revolutionary principles as only an aristocrat could: on what his Maurocordato in sardonic imitation calls "wild theories," and then hymns them: "Wild theories, that unite men in justice and amity! Wild theories, that gave birth and nurture to every art and every science; that even taught reason and humanity to the despot who lashed the sea! Solon! Aristides! Epaminondas! Phocion! ye are authors and abettors of wild theories!" [11] The roll call goes on.

Landor has left no long piece of consecutive reasoning on politics or on anything else. That is not the way he writes; nor is it the way he thinks, and I choose the word "thinks" advisedly. Thinking is not necessarily the sort of thing that is said to be done by philosophers in universities. Landor sees the world as consisting of individuals—that is, with the exception of France, and of Wales, perhaps, and of Florence when he is angry with it. His politics is ethics in the large, and in this conviction he joins not only Aristotle but most honest men everywhere. Landor thinks with his nerves because he has them—and with whatever else he has.

Though Landor has many qualities that lift a man out of the crowd, sometimes to descend upon them and crush them, he is, while active, not a man of action but a poet. He knows the power and glory of the heart because his own heart bows him over. With such elemental matters politics begins and ends. Landor makes Garibaldi say, "In a state well regulated there is no populace, there is a people. . . . The people are neither monsters nor clods, but evil government, in most countries, has made them little better." [12] When Landor feels he must make a choice as to which evil to attack first, he looks to see which causes the greater pain and which is nearer home. So Romilly cries out to Wilberforce that worse than the condition of slaves in the West Indies is that of the little children in the factories at home.[13] It is no doubt very impractical of Landor to have such views; they run the risk of being called esthetic politics, or politics that is forced by heart and nerves to be honest and humane.

II *Religion*

Landor was in favor of Catholic Emancipation, but not out of any tenderness for Roman Catholicism. His countless references to Catholicism are unfailingly denunciatory—except in the dialogue "Windham & Sheridan," where he is gentle with Catholics by being (as Crump suggests in his note) more historical than usual. Sometimes, as the reader has seen, Landor is pleased to write on the light side about religion, as an Italian might do. His *High and Low Life in Italy* (1837) is a funny little book of a sort that might have come out in *Punch* (it did in the *Monthly Repository*); Landor did not think highly of it, but two short quotations might clear the air:

"Confess your sins," cries the Bishop. "It is only to me."
"I confessed them to everybody when I committed them," said the Marquis; "and one fresh is worth ten stale."

And there are some memorable last words: "You have bothered me fairly into bliss." [14]

It is necessary to say, however, that Landor's deeper and more constant feelings about Catholicism, and Christianity in general, are as well expressed in the following note to "King James I and Isaac Casaubon" as anywhere else in his works:

Almost the only good, or rather almost the only cessation of evil, permitted by catholic princes is the abolition of the Jesuits, which must however be considered as merely the dismissal of old servants grown insolent. Princes still maintained and supported the Inquisition. During the period of these two institutions, more mischief has been done to mankind by their religion, than by all the other religions that have existed in the world. The Jesuits taught youth, but only to a certain and very circumscribed extent, and their principal dogma was the legitimacy of falsehood: hence knowledge and virtue have suffered worse from them than from the most profligate and ignorant of the other confraternities. [15]

Protestantism is not exactly favored; prelaty is blamed by Andrew Marvel for the violence of the Presbyterians and Anabaptists as popery is for that of the Reformers. [16] This criticism may seem to leave a few sects untouched by Landor; but, to be safe from him, they had to be as little organized and as powerless as possible. The attractions to despotism of either belief or faith make it a dangerous state of mind: "No fatal blow against the liberties of mankind or against the tranquillity of nations hath ever been aimed without religion." [17]

Ambition and greed prey upon faith from within as from without. Landor's Washington blames the fact of hierarchy for the animosities of English and Irish. They should be allowed to mind their own business and not the "business of those who fare sumptuously on their credulity." [18] The rationalistic choice of the word "credulity" causes Landor and Washington, quite in the eighteenth-century way, to explain themselves; and the explanations are those of Christian primitivists, Socinians, Deists, or atheists: "For Christianity is in itself of such simplicity, that whoever would make an Establishment of it must add imposture: and from imposture grows usurpation." We may, from Landor, elaborate on that simplicity: "Religion, I agree with you, is too pure for corporations: it is best meditated on in our privacy, and best acted on in our ordinary intercourse with mankind." [19]

The question is, what can without distaste be meditated on? Hell cannot, as we have seen; nor can the Fall of Man. For, speaking for himself in "Southey and Landor," Landor attests to the aversion he has to theology, above all to the kind found in Milton's *Paradise Lost*.[20] Shall we think how nice it would be if a few people were Christians? Landor has made sufficient use of the reverse of the cliché. Can we meditate on some of the prettier aspects of the divine? Hearken to President Du Paty: "Every good action, every good thought, every thing good, is of divine origin; but I see nothing of the divine in manifest fraud, swarming with its insects and reeking in its exposure." [21] Olympus was less exclusive, and Landor was not repelled by the fact.

Speaking kindly to Tsing-Ti, who fancies being a Christian, the Emperor of China says that "Christianity makes such men even better than they were before." "Like wine," he continues, "it brings out every humor. The ferocious it renders more ferocious, the exacting more exacting, the hypocritical more hypocritical, the austere more austere; and it lays more gracefully on the gentle breast the folded hands of devotion." [22] The last clause is an attempt by metaphor to suggest something, perhaps something very tenuous and elusive; but it fails to do more than reproduce a hackneyed posture: it suggests nothing whatever but something passive because in these fourteen words Landor does not know what he is talking about. He has nothing of the religious temperament; he knows at least what reverence is, but for him it is philosophical and leads to harmony and wisdom, not—certainly not—to acceptance or absorption.

As for the divine, he is a poet and has more respect for everything in the universe than a theologian can afford. I don't think his heart and soul was in what Du Paty said of the divine; it was a criticism of "our religion," and it does well enough in the conversation it was written for. Lucian is more convincing when he suggests to Timotheus that, if we are indeed looked after by beings wiser than ourselves, they must be very imperfect ones, "who indulge us in the commission of innumerable faults and follies for their own speculation or amusement." [23]

Landor is at heart a Greekish pagan in favor of happiness: "Pertinacity in a religion is usually in proportion to its absurdity; much also is dependent on climate. Hence the Gods of Greece and Italy are genial: the harsher stock on which they were engrafted is grown obsolete." [24] The classic tolerance of that may be matched with the following sentence from a letter of Landor's to Wordsworth. The shadow of the comment obliquely falls from the books to the subject itself: "I am disgusted at all things treating of religion, but Savonarola and Molinos are two such rich weeds that they are well worth climing [*sic*] the dunghill for." [25] Landor is a little like Norman Douglas's Mr. Keith, who always felt as if he needed a bath after talking about religion—and then went back to the wallow.

III   *Literature*

Nothing could keep Landor from the reading of Milton's *Paradise Lost*. When he puts it down, he says, he can "take up no other poet with satisfaction": "I seem to have left the music of Handel for the music of the streets, or at best for drums and fifes." Though he resorted to it "more for the music than the doctrine there," it offered him a combination of experiences: "I recur to it incessantly as the noblest specimen in the world of eloquence, harmony, and genius." [26]

Much of Landor's response is to epic grandeur and to capaciousness of mind. He had grown to manhood in the company of Classical authors in whose world the petty had no place, and small things were either elegantly self-contained or meant to be evocative of essences of nature itself. Literature reminded mankind of the dignity of which men were capable; with the pleasures of poetry, it offered the pleasures of study. The eighteenth century, in which Landor lived his first twenty-five years, preserved unconsciously, in the idiom of its time, an ancient Classical way of referring to serious, even strenuously intellectual, voluntary occupations as "amusing" and "delightful." "Delight" for us continues to imply a civilized and discriminating but warm participation in experience, as does *s'amuser* in French; but in English "amusement" has taken on a flavor of detached superiority, of a smile bestowed on the trivial. In "Marcus Tullius and Quinctus Cicero," we find within a few lines of each other the opinion of Cornelia that "There is no amusement so lasting and varied, so healthy and peaceful, as horti-culture"; and of Quinctus that "of all studies, the most delightful and the most useful is biography." [27]

The tone is not that of a man writing for the new age; it is not only Neoclassical, it is from beyond the Styx. And yet to say that the world of liberal education, of the independent studious gentleman, the amateur, is dead, is also to raise the question whether there ever was such a world, whether the world was not always a larger, more miscellaneous, more ferociously free-ranging phenomenon than his-torians like to pretend; whether the independent studious gentleman, the amateur, was not always a great rarity, the thought of whom was preserved for ages as an ideal by a few; and whether even now, when schooling and writing and study have become the property of the marketplace, a few may not find themselves drawn to voluntary occupations as amateurs are said to have been, each for love of the thing, for the way it delights and nourishes the body and the mind.

In Landor, there are innumerable reminders of a long tradition. Sometimes their bearing is more conservative than traditional, re-minding the average reader of the old-fogey aspects of Neoclas-sicism. "Are we not a little too fond of novelty and experiment," he asks Southey in the first of his letters to him, "and is it not reason-able to prefer those kinds of versification which the best poets have adopted and the best judges have cherished for the longest time?" [28]

Such a preference is reasonable, certainly, and that means nothing to a man who would rather be original. According to tradition, the original is not likely to be worth much, considering how long we human beings have been scratching our heads and rocking them in our hands. But we know what to think of those who are fond of referring to the past, and even if Landor did at twenty-five publish in free verse what he pretended to be translations from Arabic and Persian poetry, it was, if apparently a very avant-garde kind of behavior, a very old-fashioned one as well, at least as old as *Ossian,* who moved the dried souls of a metronomic generation. It will do Landor no good with us that to him the word "classical" is not concerned with something over and done with, as may be seen in his letter to Emerson, in which he calls Alfieri "the most classical and animated poet existing in the present or past century"; besides, he has so little of the proper modern spirit in him that he refers to Michelangelo's *Last Judgment,* in the Sistine Chapel, as a "prodigious *giblet pie.*" [29] And we know he was bored with Dante.

We can understand Landor better if we listen, for instance, to some words of his about Browning: " 'A very great poet,' he wrote in 1845, 'as the world will have to agree with us in thinking.' He only wished that Browning would 'atticize' a little. 'Few of the Athenians had such a quarry on their property, but they constructed better roads for the conveyance of the material.' " [30] Landor is not referring to style as he does once in speaking about pastoral poetry: "The thoughts of our poets in the Elizabethan age often look the stronger because they are complicated and twisted. We have the boldness to confess that we are no admirers of the Elizabethan *style.*" [31]

Any supposed "classicism" in his criticism of Browning is practicality, a respect for decent building. All good artists have it; the difference is not in quality or in kind but in what example each artist first thinks of when the subject of decent building is raised. Thus the virtue of loyalty remains itself, while the face of the loyal friend glows variously in a hundred minds: black, yellow, white, brown, bearded, smooth, oval, angular, round, childish, warmly lined and shadowed, frostbitten with experience. It is sensitivity to literature that first attracts Landor to Browning, for, on the surface, they are worlds apart; and it makes Browning feel as strongly about Landor. Sensitivity to literature? Sensitivity to life.

The *Imaginary Conversations* do not show Landor to be a reader of limited sympathies. In his own person, he declares, "There is nothing in the ruins of Rome which throws so chilling a shadow over the heart as the monument of Keats." [32] He makes Porson say that Byron "possesses the soul of poetry, which is energy" and, appreciatively, that Crabbe "wrote with a twopenny nail, and scratched rough truths and rogues' facts on mud walls." [33] He has good words for Fielding, Smollett, and Sterne, and for Richardson who, according to Landor's Alfieri, "might teach even Englishmen fine manners, and Clarissa might draw tears from them. But they think it manly to be rude, and womanly to be sensitive." [34] (Both sentences fit as easily into the nineteenth century as into the eighteenth.)

Landor pays Donne the compliment of imitating him without parody.[35] As for Cervantes, according to Landor as well as to his president Du Paty, Cervantes "had the good taste, not to say the prudence, to avoid the continuity of allegory in so long a work, and to make it yield to character." [36] Of allegory, Landor's Lucian had said that "a great poet in the hours of his idleness may indulge" in it, but that "the highest poetical character will never rest on so unsubstantial a foundation." [37] This is a poet speaking; let the mechanics of criticism try to prove him wrong. When he himself indulged in it in the dream of Petrarca at the end of the *Pentameron,* the result was pretty enough.

What Landor admires in prose, from the ancient world to the modern, appears to be most of what there is to admire. On one side is his experience that "prose on certain occasions can bear a great deal of poetry" (he says that there is as much prose in the poetry of Wordsworth, whom he reverences but does not worship, "as there is of poetry in the prose of Milton").[38] We have the prose of Milton, then, on one hand; on the other, we may put the prose of Le Sage: "Show me any style in any language so easy, so diversified." [39] Le Sage's "elegance, purity, and variety never have been and never will be exceeded." [40] Easy, yet elegant; pure, yet various —the ideal is traditional, yes; what other ideal could be imagined for the medium?

But the ideal does not describe the prose of Milton or of Carlyle, of Jeremy Taylor or of Ruskin; it could not, for we cannot specify for individual genius. Nor could we add without absurdity that an ideal prose should be passionate yet controlled, for we assume control, in both senses of the phrase, and temperament is individually bestowed. Landor's admiration of the prose of Le Sage is that of a man who knows and loves his art. There was nothing obvious about the choice, and, as for his reasons, which are a description of the ideal—anything so nearly universal in its beauty and utility is Classical. His appreciation of Milton's prose may as well be called Romantic, for the prose itself may be: the sweep of it, the excitement, and the individualistic refusal to accommodate the listener, the sense the listener has of intruding upon the grand dissonances and harmonies of a strong and tortuous mind.

As for the later prose writers, not including contemporaries, the best, Landor says, are Samuel Johnson "in his *Lives of the Poets,"* Goldsmith, Sir William Blackstone, and Sir Joshua Reynolds.[41] In each of them is the requirement of ease: Blackstone as inviting as the subject and a master of it can be, and Reynolds full of small (but elegant) surprises. Especially in Johnson's *Lives* is ease a triumph of the mind, that turns the turbulence of a lifetime into music. In Goldsmith, it is nature. Clarity, grace they all share; but the variety of Goldsmith goes unfelt by almost all readers, so swift and subtle are the changes. Why Gibbon is not in the list, even a lover of him must know: it was his own particular prose, his own mind he was master of.

The Romantic temperament may be too restless even to read such writers, Goldsmith excepted. Landor has no such limitations, is not so easily tagged. To him "the richest jewel that poetry ever wore" is from *Paradise Lost*: " 'Yielded with coy submission, modest pride, And sweet, reluctant, amorous delay.' I would rather have written these two lines than all the poetry that has been written since Milton's time in all the regions of the earth." [42] And there is a poem of Shelley's that Landor would "rather have written . . . than all that Beaumont and Fletcher ever wrote, together with all of their contemporaries, excepting Shakspeare" [43]: "Music, when soft voices die." What Landor feels so strongly about is not of a school, an age, a mood, a bias—it is poetry.

Yet there may be principles at the bottom of it, though principles cannot produce it, and vital as they are to Landor, they are very old. They look no older than they did in the most ancient of days, and that is why they may be called principles rather than tenets. Some degree of order in one's feelings, for instance, must come before there can be order in one's art. "If you turn your mind to poetry," Landor writes to Miss Rose Paynter, in 1840,

let me for once have influence enough with you to persuade you not to indulge in any kind of it which verges on sadness. . . . Take my word for it, if we fondle and pamper our griefs, they grow up to an unwieldly size and become unmanageable. Melancholy, which was at first only the ornament of a verse, becomes at last a habit and a necessity. Much of our subsequent life depends on the turn we ourselves give to the expression of our early feelings. But why am I saying all this to you? to you whose philosophy is so much sounder and surer than mine? It is because we all require to be told as often of what we know as of what we do not know. [44]

With order and control, we can make a beginning. What is the purpose of poetry or prose? The answers "poetry or prose" or "self-expression" or even "communication" would have been rejected in the days before the arts hardened their hearts against humanity because the machine was useful; "what kind?" and "for what purpose?" and "with what effects?" still seemed questions of import to be asked about any sort of project. To Landor, as to all sane men before and after him, "All the imitative arts have delight for the principal object." [45] But Landor, like his forebears, asks that they do us good; and thus he adds the principle of utility. In this respect, he would not make a good Romantic, but neither do the best Romantics. A good composition, says Vittoria Colonna, is useful, has wisdom in it: "The beautiful in itself is useful, by awakening our finer sensibilities, which it must be our own fault if we do not often carry with us into action. A well ordered mind touches no branch of intellectual pleasure so brittle and incompliant as never to be turned to profit." [46]

In a note to "Henry VIII and Anne Boleyn," Landor applies the principle of utility. "Literature and religion seem to have been contending two hundred years, unintermittingly, which of them should be most efficient in banishing humanity and civility from the world—the very things which it was their business to propagate and preserve, and without which they not only are useless but pernicious." [47] What country would he be most welcome in today?

The moral uses of art are not very well known among us except in caricature or propaganda. A mature and civilized writer could once discuss didacticism in this fashion (Landor was writing more hastily than in the *Conversations*):

A good epic, or a good tragedy, or a good comedy, will inculcate many morals; but if any poem should rest on one only, it would soon become tedious and insufferable. . . .
In the Odyssea [Homer] shows that everything yields to constancy and perseverance, but he does not *propose* to show it, and there are other morals not less obvious. Why should the whole machinery of the largest poem be brought out to establish a truth, which a single verse would inculcate more plainly and more memorably? [48]

Landor calls Boileau wise in saying—and in saying of poetry—that nothing is beautiful but what is true.[49] Well, we learn from all we hear; we bear the mark of all we have undergone. To speak truth or falsehood is to inculcate either. This recognition is what is behind the ancient principle that poetry not only delights us but instructs. The responsibility of the writer is to what is true and to what is good for us as human beings. Beauty is the signature of what human needs approve. We do not thirst against nature.

Landor also has some technical advice for us, based firmly on a knowledge of what it is like to read. Lord Chatham is talking: "It appears, then, to me that elegance in prose composition is mainly this: a just admission of topics and of words; neither too many nor too few of either; enough of sweetness in the sound to induce us to enter and sit still; enough of illustration and reflection to change the posture of our minds when they would tire; and enough of sound matter in the complex to repay us for our attendance." [50] The truth to physical experience is so happily phrased as to constitute an invitation to literature.

As a rule, however, his literary principles are, as they must be, brief and unparticularized. The widely held opinion that Plato is eloquent causes him to say, through Diogenes, that there is no eloquence "where there is no ardour, no impulse, no energy, no concentration. Eloquence raises the whole man: thou raisest our eyebrows only." [51] Lucian returns to the subject: "Tell me over and over that you find every great quality in Plato: let me only once ask you in return, whether he ever is ardent and energetic, whether he wins the affections, whether he agitates the heart." [52]

Heart, then, as well as mind, must be satisfied. In great poetry, Landor says, the greatest qualities are invention, vigor, directness, and enthusiasm.[53] The movements of great writers—like those of Pindar, Horace, Milton, and Shakespeare—are "as easy as they are vigorous." [54] "Every good writer has much idiom; it is the life and spirit of language." [55] But such ease and freedom do not fall into diffuseness or obscurity: "The poetical form like the human, to be beautiful, must be succinct." [56] "Perspicuity," says Landor's Epicurus, "is the prime excellence of composition." [57] And his Lucian: "In my opinion all philosophers should speak clearly. The highest things are the purest and brightest; and the best writers are those who render them the most intelligible to the world below." [58] Landor does not insist that verse be as perspicuous as prose; without opening the door to obscurity, he acknowledges the difference in kinds of experience: that in the best poetry there may be "an undersong of sense" [59] not heard or understood but by those of poetical mind.

The principles of literature, as Landor sees them, are those of a beneficiary of Greece and Rome, and of the best work done in

Northern Europe down to his own time. Those principles are strongly flavored with Hellenism. They are about as universal as principles can be, if the universe extends from the Aegean to the Tyrrhenian and north to somewhere along the western coast of Scotland.

CHAPTER 6

Style and Substance

"DINNER was elaborately simple," said Carlyle of his visit to Landor at Bath in July, 1850. "The brave Landor was really stirring company: a proud, irascible, trenchant, yet generous, veracious, and very dignified old man; quite a ducal or royal man in the temper of him. . . ." [1] The word "veracious" contrasts with an earlier remark that "Landor is a man of real capacity for literary work of some sort, but he has fallen into an extravagant method of stating his opinions, which makes any serious acceptance of them altogether impossible." Yet Carlyle had then to add that "there was something honorable and elevated, too, in his views." [2]

It was equally natural for Landor to notice the extravagance of Carlyle in his public letter to Emerson, in 1856: "I have enjoyed the conversation of Carlyle within the room where I am writing. It appeared at that time less evidently than now that his energy goes far beyond his discretion. Perverseness is often mistaken for strength, and obstinacy for consistency. There is only one thing in which he resembles other writers, namely, in saying that which he can say best, and with most point." [3] The last sentence shows understanding of literature; it is from there that we may go on to a judgment of a man and his work.

But, to round out Carlyle's portrait of Landor at Bath, take a sentence or two from Monckton Milnes: "While Landor's wilful temper was making himself and all about him unhappy, the innermost man, as reflected in his books, was yearning for a condition of things where all was courtesy and peace. No one could see him in high and refined society without being impressed by a dignified grace, which is just what a student of his writings would have expected from his style." [4] See him in civilized society: even if there were only two people in his unpretentious lodgings. Perhaps this grace of style must be won to, through frenzy itself; perhaps it is possible only if, as we must suppose was true of the hot-tempered Greeks, the peace of it is deeply enough desired.

There are those, however—the majority, perhaps—who, though they can quote something to the effect that a man and his style are one and the same, are able to conceive of style and matter as having no connection with each other. People will grant to a Landor something called good prose or even beautiful style but go on to say that its content is of no particular value to a man of intelligence. That is a view of the good and the beautiful to end all views and deliver the city to the wolves. "We feel," intones Sir Leslie Stephen —and mental spongers have by now increased the number of him from the editorial arrogance of two to many—"that the most super-human of schoolboys has really a rather shallow view of life." [5] Are "we" really as profound as that? And so thunderously adult?

By "shallow view of life" people usually turn out to have meant some kind of materialism: a high valuation (how high?) put upon money or power or social position (that is not Landor's trouble); or, what such people appear to consider a much more deadly thing, a love of this life and this world, a preference for what is concrete and intimately knowable over what is abstract and merely to be conceived of; and a more or less instinctive conviction that what is worth working for is happiness. This conviction is so deeply consonant with human physiology and with human nature in general that those to whom our world is a lie can condemn it out of hand as shallow. What is true and profound to them is not available to the senses: such a view saves them the occasional embarrassment of confessing that they hate life. There are probably not many such people, but their way of thinking has formed the state of things we know, and the rest of us would feel lost if we could not recite our litany together.

Landor had thrown down the glove to his critics in "Diogenes and Plato" (1829) when he gave poor Plato something to defend himself with, for as long as it took to say it:

. . . it became you to demonstrate where and in what manner I had made Socrates appear less sagacious and less eloquent than he was; it became you likewise to consider the great difficulty of finding new thoughts and new expressions for those who had more of them than any other men, and to represent them in all the brilliancy of their wit and in all the majesty of their genius. I do not assert that I have done it; but if I have not, what man has? what man has come so nigh to it? He who could bring Socrates, or Solon, or Diogenes, through a dialogue, without disparagement, is much nearer in his intellectual powers to them, than any other is near to him.[6]

"Without disparagement": the question is whether Landor was fit to speak in the name of all these celebrated persons. The fact that he spoke through them mainly for himself was a risk the more— and, if he passed safe, the more the glory. It is not thought by critics that his Diogenes, his Cicero, his Lucian, and the rest are intellectually inferior to the originals. What, then, are the dissatisfied people unable to make clear about their own dissatisfaction? Perhaps Saintsbury speaks for some of them when he declares that "in any kind of reasoning proper," Landor is "as an infant in arms." Would Saintsbury grant reasoning proper to Montaigne (speaking of monologists)? Is reasoning proper a thing we should expect to find in a literary piece called a "Conversation"? And then comes the left-handed compliment that Landor had "nothing particular to say, with a matchless faculty for saying anything," [7] with its picture of Landor matchlessly winging through the inane.

I suppose there is no settling the matter. "He has nothing (or something) to say" is a grunt of dissatisfaction (or satisfaction) descriptive of the man who emits it, though the negative is always safer, what with the littleness of human things and its sharp-edged, decisive tone of infinite experience. If nothing can be proved, we may be able to come a little closer than we are now to the nature of Landor's work.

Landor felt the need to say something about himself and his art, and he did so in 1848 in words he put into the mouth of the Princess Belgioioso:

King. It is a relief to change the subject a little from politics and battles. No subject can support a long-continued conversation, excepting love.

Princess. Love also is the fresher for a short excursion. Seldom do I read a dialogue, even by the cleverest author, without a sense of weariness. Sentences cut up into question and answer on grave subjects, into repartee on lighter, are intolerable. Such is the worst method of instructing a child, or of attracting a man or woman. And there is something very absurd in the supposition that any abstruse question, or matter of deep thought, can be shuffled backward and forward in this off-hand manner. Even where the discourse is upon a subject the most easy and tractable, we are fond of departing from the straight level walk to some narrower alley that diverges out of it; and we always feel the cooler and pleasanter in passing out of one room into another.[8]

The femininity of the princess is unassailable. But, under the splintered glancing of her mind, under her busy inattention, hides an author of unread books. Unread, although he too is "fond of departing from the straight level walk," he diverges by nature into a pleached alley and then into a sunny field; he climbs a stile; he lies down under a tree. If people have not followed him there, it has been because they wanted excitement and the kind of talk they were accustomed to, and they found these in a pub in the village.

His fondness for divagation and for peaks of pause in the talk ought to tell us a great deal about him. In prose, as in verse, he is not a laborious builder of large things, nor a quick sketcher of hints, but a maker of sentences, small things that may be perfect. If they are beautiful, they are not empty; if they are even good, they are equally meaningful; that is, they are of use. In prose, as in verse, Landor has a bent toward aphorism, many examples of which have already been quoted in these pages, though buried in longer passages. They are often short maxims, generalizations struck off by the kind of mind that likes to clear the air now and then or sweep the hoarded rubbish off a desk: "Temperance and beneficence contain all other virtues." [9] And: "We must never say all we think, and least so in poetry." [10]

The first of these is what bright reviewers nowadays sneer at as "so-called wisdom." What do they prefer to it? It is a simple statement, so bald and plain that the verb may, by impatient readers, be taken for another, and the metaphor and all its meaning missed. It is still not a very original sentence, but it is probably a true one, and of the sort that has to be hammered at us every day or so, lest we lose the desire to be wise and settle down to torturing ourselves and others. The second maxim's reminder that reticence is an important principle in life and art is something else to be welcomed by the quiet reader and scorned by the wild one; it is a Classical principle, of course, discovered and preserved by people who had so much natural energy and exuberance that they did not have to seek for it neurotically and woo it in Romantic art; they boiled over so easily that restraint rose out of the steam as a virtue needing no argument.

It may be rather shallow of Landor's Peterborough to say that "All the rogues that ever lived have brought little misery upon the world, in comparison with those who had too much zeal." [11] In the end, we may find something more vicious masquerading as zeal; but the aphorism is a vigorous and pleasant one, and it is particularly welcome after a little reading in the history of the century in which Peterborough was born.

The meaning of such sentences rebounds like an echo, or like a handball, as if meanings ought to be free, not walled in by words. Still in the same vein of casual discovery, but with an open door at the end, and a vista, is this criticism of society: "Cities are ignorant that nothing is more disgraceful to them than to be the birth-places of the illustriously good, and not afterward the places of their residence; that their dignity consists in adorning them with distinctions, in intrusting to them the regulation of the commonwealth, and not in having sold a crust or cordial to the nurse or midwife." [12] This essay in ethics and politics could be played by the brasses. In the sober movements of its parallel ideas, the splendid force of its alliteration and assonance, and the perfectly controlled and ornamental epigrammatic contempt at the end, it is the rebuke of a man whose stature is above cities.

To turn from a public Landor who cannot easily be forgotten, here is the preface to a more private one, in words of Diogenes to philosophers: "The intellectual world, like the physical, is inapplicable to profit and incapable of cultivation a little way below the surface,—of which there is more to manage, and more to know, than any of you will undertake." [13] This idea can be called profound (if the word must be bestowed at all) not because it is obscure, not because it is metaphysical—it is neither—but because its neglected common sense, its flouted truth, is endlessly rich in possibilities for human life. We have heard Landor before on the importance of the concrete. From our housekeeping in the midst of it, our truth and our poetry arise. And so the most characteristic of Landor's best sentences reflect the natural growth of our thoughts in being themselves a collaboration of the senses: "The human heart is the world of poetry: the imagination is only its atmosphere." [14] Many are grave or deep-toned: "The noble mansion is most distinguished by the beautiful images it retains of beings past away; and so is the noble mind"; [15] or "The children of Niobe fell by the arrows of Diana under a bright and cloudless sky." [16] Here, by a clarion assonance, Niobe, Diana, and the bright sky burn together in a second and ultimate irony.

In another key—and how caressingly addressed to the ear and to the pulse—we find: "The morning comes, the fresh world opens, and the vestiges of one are trodden out by many: they were only on the dew, and with the dew they are departed." [17] Landor has been able not only to perceive but subtly to seize more than a few of what he calls "those innumerable filaments of thought which break as they rise from the brain." [18] They are of various colors, as one instance after another would show: "In courts, where silliness alone escapes suspicion, we must shake false lights over the shallows, or we shall catch nothing." [19]

Even words that burst from him, evidences of the irascible or simply the opinionated individualist, may show cousinship to the ones above, as do these in a letter to G. P. R. James, April 22, 1839, in which Landor is referring to the neighborhood of Hampton Court: "I hear there are many new houses built near the palace. I hate all new things—all without exception, except a swallow nest." [20] This ejaculation too belongs to what Swinburne called Landor's "rapid thought and radiant utterance." [21] His four words are exact; Swinburne knew what he had been listening to—and knew that radiance had not been pre-empted for all time by Shelley.

What critics might agree to settle for is just the fact that Landor is a poet: not a poet-philosopher, like Plato; not a poet-prophet and poet-historian, like Carlyle; but a man to whom almost any instant of experience is worth squeezing for its essence in soul-delighting words. No single subject absorbs him as does all his living, and he must sing what he finds to say about it. Song starts at the toes and fingertips.

We have heard more than once of the busyness of Landor's mind out-of-doors; the character of this bristly man's marriage with life is defined by his poetry; it is suggested also by these words in a letter to Wordsworth: "The principal thing that keeps my pen idle, is, the unwillingness I feel to disturb, by any motion but walking, the ideas that come and take their pastime . . . colours and motions I wish, unless I try to catch & detain them. I am naturally fond of letting any thing run to waste, and am as reluctant to write down a thought as I am to cut a flower from a shrub and stick it in my button-hole." [22] A touch of exaggeration by way of seasoning is to be understood; he was, after all, quick to record a thought. Yet in

his own muscular way he may have known something of a Joubert-
ian languor, which not only absorbs the slightest tremors around it
but quietly fashions them into meaning. Landor's reverential idleness is a praise of all creation. Nothing of it, as he well knew, not
a whiff of it went to waste. Our memory inhabits our whole frame.
And the contemplative man has an animal alertness in repose.

The variety of Landor's music is not well enough known. I do
not instance his *Citation and Examination of William Shakespeare,*
a romp at book length on the matter of deer-stealing, for stylistically
he has laced himself into the costume of an Elizabethan. How, he
asks himself, would not just Sir Thomas Lucy and the rest, but
young Will Shakespeare actually have spoken—if snared in
comedy? It is breezy, it is rambunctious; unlike some readers, I
would say it deserves to be called a tour de force; but whether it
succeeds or fails with any reader, it is not Landor except that he
did it. His love of language had an Elizabethan side to it; of that we
were not unaware. The extent to which he could indulge that side
of him is what the fact of his writing the *Citation* tells us.

For his variety in mastery, above all for his range, we may
observe Landor composing instead in the Phrygian mode: "I have
known one hoisted up from the grave's edge by sticking manfully to
the neck of a boar. Venison is sheepish; boar for me! I can eat it
without honey and vinegar. . . ." [23] Then we may suddenly turn to
the end of Petrarch's Dream, to his glimpse of Love, far up in the
direction where Death was pointing: "I looked: the earth was under
me: I saw only the clear blue sky, and something brighter above
it." [24]

In those two passages we have gone from raw life to transfigura-
tion. Rare meat in literature seldom has the flavor of that first passage. That "hoisted," that "sticking"!—and the full-bodied, tough
whimsicalness ending in a touch of secret poetry, more intimate
than the far, cool, supernal, yet rather familiar mystery in the next
sentence. Landor knows how to sing on the heights; there is a
moment of steadying, and then in a rush comes a revelation of the
experience, not the thing revealed, in the almost childlike words
that are all we have in the presence of sublimity.

The last passage was rarified: I think that for the best things we
always have to come down a bit. Degrees of fineness, degrees of
perfection are not easy to calculate above eye-level. In this passage
we are in our own world: "There is a gloom in deep love, as in

deep water: there is a silence in it that suspends the foot." With these words I would end a perfect utterance, but it goes on, after a semicolon, beautifully: "and the folded arms and the dejected head are the images it reflects. No voice shakes its surface: the Muses themselves approach it with a tardy and a timid step, and with a low and tremulous and melancholy song." [25] Fancy, in other words, took it up where imagination left it. What else was possible? Down to the suspended foot it was consummate poetry. How after that to pick up the thread of even eloquent discourse; how to descend from that star? Landor made his descent in a slow dance of syllables, while discourse waited, as in decency it had to do, in silence, until, after another sentence, the lingering music was gone.

The best known of his prose passages is music *in excelsis*. It is as free-standing and unapologetic as "O World! O Life! O Time!" It contains a similitude of genius, and a final sentence that turns the body of the reader into a viol:

> Laodameia died; Helen died; Leda, the beloved of Jupiter, went before. It is better to repose in the earth betimes than to sit up late; better, than to cling pertinaciously to what we feel crumbling under us, and to protract an inevitable fall. We may enjoy the present while we are insensible of infirmity and decay: but the present, like a note in music, is nothing but as it appertains to what is past and what is to come. There are no fields of amaranth on this side of the grave; there are no voices, O Rhodopè, that are not soon mute, however tuneful; there is no name, with whatever emphasis of passionate love repeated, of which the echo is not faint at last. [26]

In the prose passages that Landor works on as if they were separate creations there is as a rule an increase in tenseness or poignancy, often finer and finer, into the cadence, the slow fall, the controlled relaxation of finality; and, answering one of the needs of our nature, the completest music is likely to proceed in a system of threes, as in the sentence beginning "There are no fields of amaranth."

On another subject, we hear another kind of music. Edward I says to Wallace that it must have been hard to be forced all along the road barefoot and bareheaded in the snow:

> *Wallace.* Not that, indeed; for I went barefooted in my youth, and have mostly been bareheaded when I have not been in battle. But to be thrust and shoven into the courtyard; to shiver under the pent-house from which the wind had blown the thatch, while the blazing fire within made the snow upon the opposite roof redden

like the dawn; to wax faint, ahungered, and athirst, when, within arm's length of me, men pushed the full cup away, and would drink no more,—to that I had never been accustomed in my country.[27]

A dramatist adapts language to character and circumstances; a stylist composes for them. Here are the "thrust" and "shoven" of rude physical action; we have learned to count on Landor for words that set our own muscles working, that make fists rather than describe them. After the first full phrase, setting the conditions of a long sentence, the strong man climbs the hill of his anger that grows with each breath he takes. The breathing is quick, but he pulls deep on his lungs. The third section of the sentence seems (rightly for the rise of feeling) longer than the second, for more thoughts are rammed into it than into the second; and there are more short pauses where the broad breast heaves for pride of life. This aria is for a big voice. It plays faster and faster upon the ear until the climax—until enough has been said—and then the cadence that is no fall.

For variety of tempo and tone color, and for all the exquisite pleasures of its prose, I submit a few moments in the presence of Filippo Lippi, who throbs with no little of the life of Landor:

While I continued in that country, although I was well treated, I often wished myself away, thinking of my friends in Florence,—of music, of painting, of our villegiatura at the vintage-time; whether in the green and narrow glades of Pratolino, with lofty trees above us, and little rills unseen, and little bells about the necks of sheep and goats, tinkling together ambiguously; or amid the gray quarries, or under the majestic walls of ancient Fiesole; or down in the woods of the Doccia, where the cypresses are of such girth that, when a youth stands against one of them, and a maiden stands opposite, and they clasp it, their hands at the time do little more than meet. Beautiful scenes, on which Heaven smiles eternally, how often has my heart ached for you! He who hath lived in this country can enjoy no distant one. He breathes here another air; he lives more life; a brighter sun invigorates his studies, and serener stars influence his repose. Barbary hath also the blessing of climate; and, although I do not desire to be there again, I feel sometimes a kind of regret at leaving it. A bell warbles the more mellifluously in the air when the sound of the stroke is over, and when another swims out from underneath it, and pants upon the element that gave it birth. In like manner, the recollection of a thing is frequently more pleasing than the actuality: what is harsh is dropped in the space between.[28]

The substance is life lived and life observed, following in speed and sensuous quality the memory of it moving through the veins.

Even a sentence of ordinary information, a fact of topography, Landor phrases in such a way as to make us wonder if anything should ever be written down at all if it does not really matter to the writer: "In the beautiful little town of Prato, reposing in its idleness against the hill that protects it from the north, and looking over fertile meadows, southward to Poggio Cajano, westward to Pistoja, there is the convent of Santa Margarita." [29] This picture is something creatively seen; what we learn is carefully placed before us, touched with affection, delicately adjusted; and then the creator steps back a little, his hands still poised from the balance he has made. The craftsmanship is generous and fond, as was the gift of room and time in the mind; the pace is noble in its deliberate ease. Nothing much had to be said in the first place, if it had not been that between speaker and subject there was a fruitful concord. Prato was sung into being, and the convent found itself there.

In Landor's work I am not conscious of the craftsman's labor; there is an inner rightness as if the ear were an instant judge, though the outlying form may lack proportion. He strokes his words as he chooses them, and fondles them as they pass. The life of his work is in the sentence; he improves the shining moment—and innumerable such moments are his immortality. In prose and verse he is a deeply pagan poet, and his pages are an epicure's feast. His love of musical speech communicates itself so strongly that the attentive reader of his prose is more conscious of harmony—of the music of word and idea together—than he is of the person speaking or of the author behind him.

"You heard no breath/Outside the flute," said Landor of the old Greeks.[30] The prose of our other great makers, whether a Browne or a Taylor, a Carlyle or a Ruskin, even a Swift or a Johnson, impresses us with themselves; we feel the weight of them in their sentences. Landor escapes; we are conscious of mastery, not of the presence of a master. As a bird performing high in the air may strike us less as a bird than as flight itself, so Landor is marvelously prose. He is the only such master we have. Everything else we have credited to him is of a more earthly nature.

Music is an endless quest, and the music Landor arrived at in his work, as in his life, was not perfect; but he knew how much of his work was good to behold, how much of it reflected knowledge and self-command in the craftsman and a heart that was early drawn to Apollo, to learn repose in the heat of light:

> Wearers of rings and chains!
> Pray do not take the pains
>   To set me right.
> In vain my faults ye quote;
> I write as others wrote
>   On Sunium's hight.[31]

Though abstemious as a Greek, he could call Maenads by name. He was not unacquainted with the Furies. "Classical," he knew, was an ideal, not an accident of history or a school with a necktie of its own.[32] Greece, however, might be a lifelong orientation:

> Greece with calm eyes I see,
> Her pure white marbles have not blinded me,
>   But breathe on me the love
> Of earthly things as bright as things above:
>   There is (where is there not?)
> In her fair regions many a desert spot;
>   Neither is Dircè clear,
> Nor is Ilissus full throughout the year.[33]

There it is, the lovely melody, and with it the unmistakable mark of his genius, his finality of phrase.

"I *am* romantic," he once said to Southey.[34]

Of course. And only a classic artist could have achieved his passionate calm.

Notes and References

All quotation from Landor's works is from the following editions unless otherwise noted.

"Crump": *Imaginary Conversations by Walter Savage Landor,* with bibliographical and explanatory notes by Charles G. Crump. 6 vols. (London, 1891).

"Crump Longer": *The Longer Prose Works of Walter Savage Landor,* edited with notes and index by Charles G. Crump (London, 1892-93).

"Wheeler": *The Poetical Works of Walter Savage Landor,* edited by Stephen Wheeler. 3 vols. (Oxford, 1937).

Chapter One

1. *Complete Works of Ralph Waldo Emerson,* Centenary Edition (Boston, 1904), Vol. 12, p. 340.

2. (To James Russell Lowell, January [?] 1870 [?]) *The Letters of Ralph Waldo Emerson,* ed. Ralph L. Rusk (New York, 1939), Vol. VI, p. 100.

3. John Forster, *Walter Savage Landor, a Biography* (London, 1869), Vol. II, p. 220.

4. R. H. Super, *Walter Savage Landor, a Biography* (New York, 1954), p. 490.

5. *Ibid.,* pp. 430-31.

6. Leslie Stephen, "Landor's Imaginary Conversations," *Hours in a Library* (London, 1907), Vol. III, p. 221.

7. A. C. Swinburne, *Letters,* ed. Cecil Y. Lang (New Haven, 1960), Vol. IV, p. 220.

8. Super, p. 509.

9. *Ibid.,* p. 508.

Chapter Two

1. Crump IV, 427.

2. Wheeler III, 383. Landor had been speaking of the "murder" of Keats, in a note to "A Satire on Satirists" (1836).

3. "The Birth of Poesy," Wheeler III, 396, ll. 217-18.

4. *Ibid.*, 400, ll. 407-12.

5. *Ibid.*, 413, ll. 181-88.

6. *Ibid.*, 427, l. 94.

7. "Apology for Satire," *Ibid.*, 417-18, ll. 5, 7, 27.

8. "Pyramus and Thisbe," *Ibid.*, 423, l. 76.

9. "Abelard to Eloise," *Ibid.*, 425, l. 8.

10. *Ibid.*, ll. 105, 107. One instance of immaturity of technique might be mentioned: "Them crystal cottages again receive," in which there is no reason for the great stress on "them," and consequently for its position and the silly effect. ("The Patriot," l. 36.)

11. "The Marten," Wheeler III, 434. Compare "meek as unfledged doves, waiting with retorted neck and reverted eye for another pea to be pushed into the beak."—"The Letters of a Conservative" (1836), Letter X: *The Complete Works of Walter Savage Landor,* ed. T. Earle Welby and Stephen Wheeler (London, 1927-36), Vol. XII, p. 218.

12. "To a Lady Lately Married," Wheeler III, 437.

13. *Ibid.*, 446, ll. 27-38.

14. Clara Reeve, *The Progress of Romance* (New York, 1930), p. 13.

15. *Gebir* (Wheeler I, 1-55), Book V, 105-18.

16. *Idem,* 129-30.

17. *Idem,* 133.

18. Book VII, 204-6.

19. *Idem,* 227-30.

20. For Shelley see Forster, II, 453; for De Quincey, his *Essays on the Poets, and Other English Writers* (Boston, 1853), p. 247.

21. *The Letters of Charles Lamb,* ed. E. V. Lucas (New Haven, 1935), I, 161.

22. Book VII, 249-52. R. D. Havens, in *The Influence of Milton on English Poetry* (Cambridge, Mass., 1922), quotes one passage from *Gebir* as Miltonic:

> Than Rhine
> What river from the mountains ever came
> More stately! most the simple crown adorns
> Of rushes, and of willows, intertwined
> With here and there a flower—[etc.] (VI, 121-132)

"The style of *Gebir* is severe," said Landor, "because when I composed it, I was fresh from repeated perusals of Pindar." (Super, 42.)

23. Lucas, II, 434. Cf. *Gebir*, IV, 205-6.

24. Book II, 238-40.

25. Book III, 236.

26. *Idem*, 281-82.

27. *Idem*, 42-43.

28. Book V, 17-18.

29. Book III, 256-57.

30. Book VI, 46.

31. Book II, 118-19.

32. Book VII, 182-86.

33. Book I, 170-77.

34. *Idem*, 227-28.

35. Forster, I, 294.

36. Forster, I, 294.

37. Thomas De Quincey, *Essays on the Poets, and Other English Writers* (Boston, 1853), p. 287.

38. *Ibid.*, p. 290.

39. (1882.) A. C. Swinburne, *Miscellanies* (London, 1886), p. 203.

40. *Count Julian* (Wheeler I, 161-224), Act IV, Sc. 1, ll. 122-25.

41. Super, 105.

42. *Count Julian*, Act V, Sc. 2, ll. 17-24.

43. Act II, Sc. 1, ll. 29-37.

44. Forster, I, 288.

45. Corneille, *Médée*, I, 5.

46. Chamfort, *Maximes et Pensées, Anecdotes et Caractères,* ed. Louis Ducros, (Paris, 1928), p. 52: "The 'Myself' of Medea has been called sublime; but whoever is unable to say the same in all the tribulations of life does not amount to much as a person—or rather amounts to zero."

47. *Count Julian*, Act V, Sc. 4, ll. 253-61.

48. *Ibid.*, Act IV, Sc. 2, ll. 94-104.

49. Forster, II, 349.

50. Forster, II, 362.

51. Forster, II, 348.

52. J. B. Hubbell, "Some New Letters of Landor," *The Virginia Magazine of History and Biography*, LI (1943), p. 291.

53. *Andrea of Hungary*, (Wheeler I, 279-341), Act I, Sc. 2, ll. 5-7.

54. *Ibid.*, Act I, Sc. 4, ll. 80-93.

55. *Ibid.*, Act V, Sc. 1, ll. 12-18.

56. *Ibid.*, Act IV, Sc. 5, ll. 31-37.

57. *Ibid.*, Act V, Sc. 2, ll. 46-50.

58. *Ibid.*, Act I, Sc. 3, ll. 20-29.

59. *Ibid.*, Act IV, Sc. 6.

60. *Ibid.*, Act V, Sc. 1, ll. 28-31.

61. *Giovanna of Naples* (Wheeler I, 341-84), Act V, Sc. 2, ll. 39-40.

62. *Fra Rupert* (Wheeler I, 384-429), Act V, Sc. 4, ll. 17-18.

63. *Giovanna of Naples,* Act IV, Sc. 2, ll. 48-49.

64. *Fra Rupert,* Act V, Sc. 1, ll. 38-43.

65. *Ibid.,* Act II, Sc. 6, ll. 48-51.

66. Oliver Elton, *A Survey of English Literature,* 1780-1880 (New York, 1920), II, p. 24.

67. Colvin, p. 187.

68. *The Siege of Ancona* (Wheeler I, 429-72), Act III, Sc. 2, ll. 47-60.

69. *Ibid.,* Act I, Sc. 4, ll. 65-67.

70. *Ibid.,* Act III, Sc. 1.

71. Crump Longer, II, 162.

72. "Ines de Castro" (Wheeler I, 225-53), Part I, ll. 490-93.

73. *Ibid.,* Part III, ll. 295-96.

74. *Ibid.,* Part II, ll. 41-42.

75. *Ibid.,* Part III, ll. 211-15.

76. "Anne Boleyn and Constable of the Tower," Wheeler I, 277, ll. 78 and 70.

77. *Ibid.,* 277, ll. 88-90.

78. *Ibid.,* 276, ll. 31-32.

79. *Ibid.,* 276, ll. 46-49.

80. "Walter Tyrrel and William Rufus," Wheeler I, 265, ll. 45-49.

81. *Ibid.,* 266, ll. 74-78.

82. "Antony and Octavius," Wheeler II, 69, ll. 38-51.

83. *Ibid.,* 70, ll. 64-65.

84. *Ibid.,* 47, ll. 183-85.

85. *Ibid.,* 67, ll. 57-64.

86. Crump Longer, I, 387. Also Wheeler, II, 79. The quotation is from his "Satire on Satirists," Wheeler, III, 385, ll. 201-2.

87. Wheeler II, 81, l. 71.

Chapter Three

1. *Poemata et Inscriptiones* (1847), p. 348. The translation is from Super, 41.

2. Wheeler II, 110, ll. 61-73.

3. Book VI, ll. 43-44.

4. "Icarios and Erigonè," Wheeler II, 163, ll. 33-39.

5. "Wrongs I have suffered," Wheeler, II, 437.

6. "Tenderest of tender hearts," Wheeler, II, 414-15.

7. "Acon and Rhodope," Wheeler II, 211, ll. 5-11.

8. "Pan and Pitys," Wheeler II, 188, ll. 50-53.

9. In the Yescombe affair he was attacking a dragon.

10. Forster, II, 514. "The Death of Paris and Oenone" is the Third Part of "Corythos" in the new version first published in 1859.

11. Wheeler, I: 158, l. 379 and 519, l. 234. (Latin poems appeared in 1815, 1820, and 1847; English versions variously in 1846, 1847, 1859, and 1863.)

12. *On Writing and Writers,* ed. George Gordon (London, 1926), p. 140.

13. Wheeler, II: 157, l. 349 and 519, l. 213.

14. Wheeler, II: 199, l. 27 and 525, l. 28. In the Latin, what is shaken is *umbra.* Generally speaking, the detail of the first English version is to be found in the Latin. "Eve's star and Love's," however, had been simply Hesperus.

15. *Ibid.,* 203, l. 194 and 528, l. 184.

16. Wheeler, II: 208, l. 182 and 532, l. 207.

17. *Ibid.,* 530, ll. 98-99.

18. *Ibid.,* 533, l. 226.

19. *Ibid.,* 531, ll. 122-29.

20. *Ibid.,* 205, l. 94 and 530, l. 98.

21. *Ibid.,* 207, l. 156 and 532, l. 180. The trembling of water, but not the whole image, he already had in the Latin.

22. Wheeler, I, 110, l. 309 and 505, l. 278.

23. *Ibid.,* 117, l. 573 and 510, l. 107.

24. *Ibid.,* 114, l. 465 and 508, l. 36. The poetry here is English; it owes nothing to Landor's Latin version.

25. Wheeler II, 126, ll. 91-105. This is a lyrical conversation. Wheeler files it under "Dramas and Dramatic Scenes," which may mean almost anything. It takes its place among our Idyls.

26. Wheeler II, 519, ll. 37-38: "impubis preme verba ferocia formae" ("Cupido et Pan. Idyllion I.")

27. "Landor's 'Hellenics,' " in Richard Aldington, *Literary Studies and Reviews* (New York, 1924), pp. 152-53.

28. Wheeler II, 236, ll. 73-82.

29. *Ibid.,* 237, ll. 109-15.

30. Wheeler III, 375.

31. Wheeler II, 315.

32. *Ibid.,* 487.

33. *Ibid.,* 463.

34. *Ibid.,* 476.

35. *Ibid.,* 406.

36. Wheeler III, 445.

37. *Ibid.,* 380, ll. 34-35 and 384, l. 149.

38. Maria da Gloria (Maria II) to Ferdinand of Saxe-Coburg. Wheeler II, 338.

39. Wheeler III, 465.

40. Or however it sounds best.

41. Wheeler III, 228.

42. *Ibid.*, 227.

43. *Ibid.*, 371.

44. "Irony," in H. W. Fowler, *A Dictionary of Modern English Usage* (Oxford, 1926).

45. Forster, II, 537.

46. Wheeler III, 134.

47. *Ibid.*, 264.

48. Wheeler II, 317.

49. Wheeler III, 259.

50. Wheeler II, 365, l. 11, and 373, l. 36. See also "The very dust is as it was before," in "Boastfully call we all the world our own" (Wheeler III, 239).

51. *Ibid.*, 311.

52. *Ibid.*, 440.

53. *Ibid.*, 436, "To Chaucer."

54. *Ibid.*, 452.

55. Wheeler III, 36.

56. Wheeler II, 378.

57. *Ibid.*, 387.

58. *Ibid.*, 391. ("To Macaulay.")

59. *Ibid.*, 250. ("Pievano Arlotto.")

60. Wheeler III, 274. ("On Epigrams.")

61. *Ibid.*, III, 358.

62. *Ibid.*, III, 359.

63. *Ibid.*, III, 359.

64. Wheeler III, 360.

65. *Ibid.*, 335.

66. *Ibid.*, 377.

67. *Ibid.*, 366.

68. *Ibid.*, 370.

69. *Ibid.*, 122.

70. *Ibid.*, 236.

71. *Historical Manual of English Prosody* (London, 1926), p. 306.

72. Wheeler III, 77.

73. *Ibid.*, 132.

74. *Ibid.*, 126.

75. *Ibid.*, 255.

76. *Ibid.*, 174-75.

77. *Ibid.*, 45: "Why do our joys."

78. *Ibid.*, 280.

79. *Ibid.*, 45: "All is not over."

80. *Ibid.*, 117: "Ianthe! you resolve."
81. *Ibid.*, 114.
82. *Letters,* ed. Cecil Y. Lang (New Haven, 1960), IV, 221-22.
83. Wheeler III, 234.
84. Wheeler II, 464.
85. *On Writing and Writers* (London, 1926), p. 143.
86. Wheeler III, 360.
87. Wheeler III, 167-69.

Chapter Four

1. Super, 355.
2. Super, 340.
3. Super, 104.
4. Introduction to "The Pentameron." Crump Longer, II, 5.
5. Crump II, 56.
6. *Imaginary Conversations of Literary Men and Statesmen* (London, 1824) I, p. xiv.
7. *Ibid.*, Second Series (1829) I, pp. xxvii-xxviii, in the five-volume edition (London, 1826-29).
8. Forster II, 450.
9. *MS* letter (University of Chicago library) quoted by Super, *The Publication of Landor's Works* (London, 1954) p. 82.
10. *Gebir* (London, 1798) p. i.
11. Forster II, 446.
12. Note to "Ines de Castro, Don Pedro, and Dona Blanca." Crump Longer II, 162.
13. *Henry Crabb Robinson on Books and Their Writers,* ed. E. J. Morley (London, 1938) I, 383.
14. Crump II, 137.
15. Crump I, 185.
16. Crump III, 341-46.
17. Crump IV, 136.
18. "Beniowski and Aphanasia," Crump V, 74.
19. Crump V, 71.
20. *Ibid.*, 72.
21. *Ibid.*, 108.
22. *Ibid.*, 113.
23. *Ibid.*, 81.
24. *Ibid.*, II, 317.
25. Forster II, 188.
26. Crump II, 319.
27. *Ibid.*, 323.
28. *Ibid.*, 320.

29. *Ibid.*, 325.
30. *Ibid.*, 325.
31. *Ibid.*, 328.
32. *Ibid.*, 330.
33. *Ibid.*, 332.
34. *Ibid.*, 331.
35. *Ibid.*, VI, 305.
36. *Ibid.*, 358.
37. *Ibid.*, 315.
38. *Ibid.*, V, 314-15.
39. *Ibid.*, 391.
40. *Ibid.*, 378.
41. *Ibid.*, II, 396.
42. *Ibid.*, V, 233, note.
43. *Ibid.*, VI, 16. I have preferred the later "my objects" to the earlier "our objects."
44. *Ibid.*, IV, 389.
45. *Ibid.*, 14.
46. *Ibid.*, 13.
47. *Ibid.*, 18.
48. *Ibid.*, 89.
49. *Ibid.*, 98.
50. *Ibid.*, 103.
51. *Ibid.*, I, 77.
52. *Ibid.*, 77.
53. *Ibid.*, 79.
54. *Ibid.*, 75.
55. *Ibid.*, 70.
56. *Ibid.*, 81.
57. *Ibid.*, 97.
58. *Ibid.*, 93.
59. *Ibid.*, V, 123.
60. *Landor,* 117.
61. (London: Walter Scott, 1886) p. ix.
62. R. R. Madden, *The Literary Life and Correspondence of the Countess of Blessington* (London, 1855) II, 357.
63. Crump I, 272.
64. *Ibid.*, 245.
65. *Ibid.*, 231.
66. *Ibid.*, 237.
67. *Ibid.*, 238.
68. *Ibid.*, 243.
69. *Ibid.*, 226.
70. Honeyman Collection, Lehigh University Library.
71. Crump III, 412.

72. *Ibid.,* 413.
73. *Ibid.,* 351.
74. *Ibid.,* 337.
75. *Ibid.,* IV, 307.
76. *Ibid.,* 318.
77. *Ibid.,* 338.
78. *Ibid.,* 349.
79. *Ibid.,* 425.
80. *Ibid.,* 422.
81. *Ibid.,* 427.
82. *Ibid.,* II, 335.
83. *Ibid.,* II, 338.
84. *Ibid.,* 339.
85. *Ibid.,* I, 281-82.
86. *Ibid.,* 303-4.
87. *Ibid.,* 330.
88. *Ibid.,* 326.
89. *Ibid.,* IV, 51.
90. *Ibid.,* 68.
91. "Lucullus and Caesar," Crump II, 16.
92. Crump IV, 363.
93. *Ibid.,* 370.
94. *Ibid.,* 373.
95. *Ibid.,* 52.
96. *Ibid.,* Longer, II, 87-88.
97. *Ibid.,* 9.
98. *Ibid.,* 112.
99. *Ibid.,* 105.
100. *Ibid.,* 105.
101. *Ibid.,* 21.
102. *Ibid.,* 104.
103. *Ibid.,* 132.
104. *Ibid.,* Longer, I, 394.
105. *Ibid.,* 243.
106. Crump Longer, I, 257.
107. *Ibid.,* 361.
108. *Ibid.,* 345.
109. *Ibid.,* 215.
110. *Ibid.,* 227.
111. *Ibid.,* 361.
112. *Ibid.,* 357.

Chapter Five

1. "Virgilius and Horatius," Crump II, 101.
2. Tories don't like me, Whigs detest;

Then in what quarters can I rest?
Among the Liberals? most of all
The liberals are illiberal.—Wheeler III, 363.

3. *Hellenics,* enlarged and completed, 1847. Wheeler II, 183.

4. Aspasia to Cleone, in *Pericles and Aspasia,* Crump Longer I, 278.

5. *The Examiner,* October 6, 1839. See Wheeler, *Letters Private and Public,* p. 252.

6. "Lopez Banos and Romero Alpuente," Crump V, 302.

7. Crump VI, 37.

8. *Ibid.,* II, 279.

9. *Ibid.,* I, 107.

10. *Ibid.,* I, 161.

11. "Maurocordato and Colocotroni." Crump V, 287.

12. "Garibaldi and Bosco." Welby III, 314.

13. Crump III, 147.

14. Welby XI, 173, 174.

15. Crump II, 173.

16. *Ibid.,* IV, 348.

17. *Ibid.,* V, 298.

18. "Washington and Franklin." Crump II, 267.

19. *Ibid.,* 273, 269.

20. Crump IV, 245.

21. "Peter Leopold and President du Paty." Crump II, 196.

22. Crump VI, 327.

23. *Ibid.,* I, 329.

24. Agricola in "Tacitus and Agricola," *Welby* II, 205.

25. R. H. Super, "Landor's Letters to Wordsworth and Coleridge," *Modern Philology,* LV, 2 (November, 1957), 79.

26. Crump IV, 245.

27. *Ibid.,* II, 48, 49.

28. Forster I, 216.

29. *Landor's Letter to Emerson* (Cleveland, 1895) pp. 58, 36.

30. Wheeler, *Letters and Other Unpublished Writings of Walter Savage Landor* (London, 1897), p. 179.

31. "The Idyls of Theocritus," Crump Longer II, 195.

32. "Archdeacon Hare and Walter Landor," Crump IV, 424.

33. "Southey and Porson," Crump III, 216.

34. "Alfieri and Metastasio," Crump V, 23.

35. "Walton, Cotton, and Oldways," Crump IV, esp. p. 171.

36. Crump II, 194.

37. *Ibid.,* I, 305.

38. *Ibid.,* IV, 420.

39. Wheeler, *Letters and Other Unpublished* [etc.], p. 200.

40. "The Abbé Delille and Walter Landor," Crump III, 288.

41. *Charles James Fox: a Commentary on His Life and Character,* by Walter Savage Landor, ed. by Stephen Wheeler (New York, 1907), p. 228.

42. "Southey and Landor" I, Crump IV, 213.

43. "Southey and Landor" II, Crump IV, 253.

44. Wheeler, *Letters of Walter Savage Landor, Private and Public* (London: Duckworth, 1899), pp. 57-58.

45. Crump I, 234.

46. "Vittoria Colonna and Michel-Angelo," Crump V, 171.

47. Crump V, 73.

48. *Fox: a Commentary.* 133-34. Written 1811-12.

49. To Miss Rose Paynter, *Letters . . . Private and Public,* p. 98.

50. "Chesterfield and Chatham," Crump II, 289.

51. Crump I, 94.

52. *Ibid.,* I, 304.

53. *Ibid.,* IV, 290.

54. *Ibid.,* 415.

55. *Ibid.,* I, 150.

56. *Ibid.,* III, 243.

57. *Ibid.,* I, 238.

58. *Ibid.,* 303.

59. *Ibid.,* 169.

Chapter Six

1. D. A. Wilson, *Carlyle at His Zenith* (1848-53) (London: Kegan Paul, 1927), p. 305.

2. *Ibid.,* 124.

3. *Landor's Letter to Emerson,* p. 46.

4. Houghton, Richard Monckton Milnes, 1st Baron, *Monographs Personal and Social,* (New York, 1873), p. 116.

5. Leslie Stephen, *Hours in a Library* (London: Smith, Elder, 1907), III, 225.

6. Crump I, 81. "Marcus Tullius and Quinctus Cicero" (1824) broaches the subject and discusses it at some length but not with such point.

7. George Saintsbury, *Essays in English Literature,* 1780-1860, Second Series (London, 1895), pp. 104, 107.

8. Crump VI, 420.

9. *Ibid.,* I, 70.

10. Forster II, 323.

11. Crump III, 69.

12. *Ibid.,* I, 61 (Sophocles to Pericles).

13. *Ibid.,* I, 86.

14. *Ibid.,* V, 180.

15. *The Pentameron,* Crump Longer II, 40.

16. Crump V, 174.

17. *Ibid.,* 175.

18. *Ibid.,* II, 50.

19. *Ibid.,* I, 43.

20. Jay B. Hubbell, "Some New Letters of Walter Savage Landor," *The Virginia Magazine of History and Biography,* LI (1943), 292.

21. "Landor," in *Miscellanies:* A. C. Swinburne, *Complete Works* (London, 1926), XIV, 292.

22. R. H. Super, "Landor's Letters to Wordsworth and Coleridge," *Modern Philology,* LV, 2 (November, 1957), 82. Letter, which reached England on June 3, 1828, is copied verbatim.

23. Prince in "Ovid and a Prince of the Getae," Welby II, 212.

24. *The Pentameron,* Crump Longer II, 137.

25. *Pericles and Aspasia, Ibid.* I, 162.

26. "Aesop and Rhodope," Crump I, 16-17.

27. *Ibid.,* II, 401.

28. *Ibid.,* II, 393-94.

29. *Ibid.,* II, 396.

30. "To the Author of *Festus,*" Wheeler II, 404.

31. *Ibid.,* II, 465.

32. See "To the Author of *Festus,*" *Ibid.,* II, 401.

33. "Why do I praise a peach," *Ibid.,* II, 465-66.

34. Forster I, 388.

Selected Bibliography

PRIMARY SOURCES

1. Selection of Works as First Published

Andrea of Hungary and Giovanna of Naples. London: Bentley, 1839.
To the Burgesses of Warwick. Warwick, 1797.
Count Julian: a Tragedy. [by W.S.L.] 1812.
Dry Sticks Fagoted. Edinburgh: Nichol, 1858.
Fra Rupert, the Last Part of a Trilogy. London: Saunders and Otley, 1840.
Gebir: A Poem, in Seven Books. [by W.S.L.] 1798.
Gebirus, Poema [Translated by the Author from English into Latin Verse.] Oxonii: R. Slatter et J. Munday, 1803.
The Hellenics of Walter Savage Landor. Enlarged and completed. London: Moxon, 1847. Heroic Idyls, etc.
Idyllia Nova Quinque Heroum atque Heroidum. Oxonii: Munday and Slatter, 1815. The first of the Idyls. These and others reprinted in *Poemata et Inscriptiones.* Londini: Moxon, 1847.
Imaginary Conversations of Literary Men and Statesmen. Vols. I-II: London: Taylor and Hessey, 1824. Vol. III: London: H. Colburn, 1828. Vols. IV-V ("Second Series, vols. 1-2") London: J. Duncan, 1829.
The Last Fruit off an Old Tree. London: Moxon, 1853. Includes verse and eighteen later conversations.
The Pentameron and Pentalogia. [n.p.] 1837.
Poems from the Arabic and Persian. With Notes by the Author of *Gebir.* Printed by H. Sharpe in Warwick; sold by Rivington in London, 1800.
The Poems of Walter Savage Landor. London: Cadell and Davies, 1795.
Poetry by the Author of Gebir. [Printed in Warwick, 1800.] London: Rivington, 1802.

2. Editions

The Works of Walter Savage Landor. London: Moxon, 1846. 2 vols.

The Works and Life of Walter Savage Landor. Ed. John Forster. London: Chapman and Hall, 1876. 8 vols.

Imaginary Conversations by Walter Savage Landor (6 vols.); *Poems, Dialogues in Verse, and Epigrams* (2 vols.); *The Longer Prose Works* (2 vols.). Ed. with bibliographical and explanatory notes by Charles G. Crump. London: Dent, 1891-93. This edition of the prose remains the best, though Welby has additional material.

The Complete Works of Walter Savage Landor. Ed. T. Earle Welby and Stephen Wheeler. London: Chapman and Hall, 1927-36. 16 vols. Vols XIII-XVI contain Wheeler's edition of the poems.

The Poetical Works of Walter Savage Landor. Ed. Stephen Wheeler. Oxford: Clarendon Press, 1937. 3 vols. A distinguished edition.

Selections from the Writings of Landor. Ed. Sir Sidney Colvin. (Golden Treasury Series.) London: Macmillan, 1882.

Imaginary Conversations. A Selection. Ed. E. de Selincourt. (World's Classics.) Oxford: Oxford University Press, 1914.

Imaginary Conversations and Poems. A Selection. Ed. Havelock Ellis. (Everyman's Library.) London: Dent, 1933.

Imaginary Conversations. Ed. R. H. Boothroyd. (Limited Editions Club.) Verona: Officina Bodoni, 1936.

The Sculptured Garland, A Selection from the Lyrical Poems of Walter Savage Landor. Ed. Richard Buxton. Wood engravings by Iain Macnab. London: The Dropmore Press, 1948.

Poems by Walter Savage Landor. Ed. Geoffrey Grigson. London: Centaur Press. 1964.

3. Bibliographies

A Bibliography of the Writings in Prose and Verse of Walter Savage Landor. Thomas James Wise and Stephen Wheeler. London: The Bibliographical Society, 1919.

The Publication of Landor's Works. R. H. Super. London: The Bibliographical Society, 1954. A study supplementary to the Wise and Wheeler bibliography.

SECONDARY SOURCES

ALDINGTON, RICHARD. "Landor's 'Hellenics.'" *Literary Studies and Reviews.* New York: Dial Press, 1924. Fresh and appreciative. Aldington is here as much the poet as the free-lance writer.

COLERIDGE, S. T. *Table Talk and Omniana.* Oxford: Humphrey Milford, 1917. Says that Landor's poems as wholes are unintelligible: there are "eminences excessively bright, and all the ground around and between them in darkness."

COLVIN, SIR SIDNEY. *Landor.* (English Men of Letters Series.) New York: Harper, 1881. The best book on Landor.

DAVIE, DONALD A. "The Shorter Poems of Landor," *Essays in Criticism, I*, 4 (October, 1951), 345-55. For Professor Davie, the poet and one of Landor's few modern critics, there is in all Landor's writing a "besetting sin" which "cancels out all his other [*sic*] virtues"; this is "a bewildering insecurity of *tone*." My quotations are exact.

DE QUINCEY, THOMAS. *Essays on the Poets, and Other English Writers*. Boston: Ticknor, Reed, and Fields, 1853. "Notes on Walter Savage Landor" (on *Gebir, Count Julian*, various dialogues) are enthusiastic. Eloquence marred by the familiar jocose long-windedness.

————. *The Note-Book of an English Opium-Eater, and Miscellaneous Essays*. Boston: Osgood, 1874. In "Milton *vs*. Southey and Landor" he pleasantly quarrels with Landor about some matters of versification.

DERRY, WARREN. *Dr. Parr, a Portrait of the Whig Dr. Johnson*. Oxford: Clarendon Press, 1966. Relatively useful for Landor's political background.

ELTON, OLIVER. *A Survey of English Literature, 1780-1880*. Vol. II. New York: Macmillan, 1920. Responsive and responsible criticism.

ELWIN, MALCOLM. *Savage Landor*. New York: Macmillan, 1941. American, wartime edition of a worthy book.

————. *Landor, a Replevin*. London: Macdonald, 1958. New draft of *Savage Landor* for publication in England. Written as "an attempt to recover Landor's character from misrepresentation, and his work from neglect." Most personal and warmly engaging treatment.

EMERSON, RALPH WALDO. *The Letters of Ralph Waldo Emerson*. Ed. Ralph L. Rusk. New York: Columbia University Press, 1939. 6 vols. Some interesting comments from one of Landor's faithful readers. (Emerson quoted Landor in his Journals as late as 1869.)

————. *Natural History of Intellect, and Other Papers. Complete Works*, Vol. XII (Centenary Edition). Ed. Edward Waldo Emerson. Boston: Houghton Mifflin, 1904. Contains the beautiful appreciative essay on Landor and the literary spirit from the *Dial* (October, 1841).

FIELD, KATE. "Last Days of Walter Savage Landor," *Atlantic Monthly*, XVII (April, May, and June, 1866), pp. 385, 540, 684. "Glimpses of the old man of Florence in the years 1859, 1860, and 1861." More discussion of his work than anecdote.

FLASDIECK, HERMANN M. "Walter Savage Landor und seine 'Imaginary Conversations.' " *Englische Studien*, LVIII (1924), 390-431. Dialogues as essentially political.

FORSTER, JOHN. *Walter Savage Landor, a Biography*. London: Chap-

man and Hall, 1869. 2 vols. Source of the other factual studies.
Endless paraphrase, however, is excruciating to read.

GILFILLAN, G. *Sketches of Modern Literature and Eminent Literary
Men* (Being a gallery of literary portraits). "Reprinted entire from
the London edition." New York: Appleton, 1846. Two vols. in
one. Six rhapsodic pages about Landor.

HENDERSON, W. B. DRAYTON. *Swinburne and Landor*. London:
Macmillan, 1918. Importance of Landor to Swinburne's mind and
art.

HORNE, RICHARD HENGIST. *A New Spirit of the Age*. New York:
Harper, 1844. Includes a highly flattering study of Landor, done
in collaboration with Mrs. Browning, then Elizabeth Barrett. "Mr.
Landor is not at all the product of the present age; he scarcely
belongs to it; he has no direct influence upon it; but he has been
an influence to some of its best teachers, and to some of the most
refined illustrators of its vigorous spirit."

LEE, VERNON. "The Rhetoric of Landor." *The Handling of Words*.
New York: Dodd, Mead, 1923. Landor as empty style and unfeel-
ing man.

MADDEN, R. R. *The Literary Life and Correspondence of the Countess
of Blessington*. London: Newby, 1855. 3 vols. Contains some of
the evidence of the deep affection and admiration Lady Blessington
and Landor had for each other.

MILNES, RICHARD MONCKTON, LORD HOUGHTON. *Monographs, Personal and Social*. New York: Holt and Williams, 1873. Anecdotal
and critical. Includes remarks by Landor on paintings in his collection—independent as usual: "Look at Andrea's truculent-faced
Madonnas and Holy Children that seem ready to fly at you."

MINCHIN, H. C. *Walter Savage Landor, Last Days, Letters and
Conversations*. Edited with explanatory comments by H. C. Minchin. London: Methuen, 1934. Particularly interesting for what it
shows of Browning and his faithful care of Landor. The book is
both painful and heartening.

PINSKY, ROBERT. *Landor's Poetry*. Chicago: University of Chicago
Press, 1968. First American academic study of length. Too much
about the supposed "use" of "devices"; but Mr. Pinsky says about
Landor one of the best things ever: that Landor was not thinking
of scholars to come—"his poems are designed to leave nothing more
to say" (p. 51).

RALEIGH, WALTER. *On Writing and Writers*. Ed. George Gordon.
London: Arnold, 1926. Almost the only beautiful original ever to
have professed English literature. Memorably perceptive observations on Landor.

ROBINSON, HENRY CRABB. *Henry Crabb Robinson on Books and
Their Writers*. Ed. E. J. Morley. London: Dent, 1938. 3 vols.

————. *The Correspondence of Henry Crabb Robinson with the Wordsworth Circle* (1808-1866). Oxford, 1927. 2 vols. Since we have Crabb Robinson and his mine of data, he is doubtless indispensable.

SAINTSBURY, GEORGE. *Essays in English Literature, 1780-1860*. Second Series. London: Dent, 1895. Saintsbury is not only fascinating to read, he is so often right that he has to be struggled against, now and then. Landor seen in the context of all literature.

————. *A History of English Prose Rhythm*. London: Macmillan, 1912. A notable experiment. Landor analyzed comparatively.

————. *A History of English Prosody*. London: Macmillan, 1923. 3 vols. A monument. Landor analyzed comparatively.

DE SELINCOURT, E. "Classicism and Romanticism in the Poetry of Walter Savage Landor." *Vorträge der Bibliothek Warburg 1930/ 1931: England und Die Antike*. Leipzig and Berlin: Teubner, 1932. Wordsworth's "sense sublime / Of something far more deeply interfused" was "simply incomprehensible" to Landor.

STEPHEN, SIR LESLIE. "Landor's Imaginary Conversations." *Hours in a Library*. Vol. III. London: Smith, Elder, 1907. 4 vols. Serious but condescending literary criticism.

SUPER, R. H. *Walter Savage Landor, a Biography*. New York: New York University Press, 1954. Probably definitive work.

————. "Landor" *The English Romantic Poets and Essayists, a Review of Research and Criticism*. Revised edition. Ed. C. W. and L. H. Houtchens. Published for the Modern Language Association of America. New York: New York University Press, 1966. Very useful for the student after he has read Landor.

SWINBURNE, ALGERNON CHARLES. *Letters*. Ed. Cecil Y. Lang. New Haven: Yale University Press, 1960. 6 vols. Of biographical and critical importance.

————. *Miscellanies*. London: Chatto and Windus, 1886. Essay on Landor reprinted from the *Encyclopaedia Britannica*, 9th edition, 1882.

SYMONS, ARTHUR. *The Romantic Movement in English Poetry*. New York: Dutton, 1909. His mixed literary impressions of Landor belong in any small gathering of commentary.

TRAILL, H. D. *The New Lucian*. Revised and enlarged edition. London: Chapman and Hall, 1900. Plato and Landor converse in the shades about the nature of Hellenism and its survival in, among others, Matthew Arnold.

VITOUX, PIERRE. *L'Oeuvre de Walter Savage Landor*. Paris: Presses Universitaires de France, 1964. Longest and most elaborate study of the works. Interested in establishing chronological continuity and unity.

WHITING, LILIAN. *The Florence of Landor*. Boston: Little, Brown,

1905. Some photographs of Landor's villa. The descriptions of the locale are over half a century out of date.

WILLIAMS, STANLEY T. "The Story of *Gebir*, XXXVI, *PMLA*, (1921), p. 615. Traces the sources of the story and compares Landor's version with Clara Reeve's.

Index